Legal and Military Reforms

Ali L. Karaosmanoğlu

Legal and Military Reforms

Secularism and Strategic Thought from the Empire to
Republican Turkey

PETER LANG

Berlin · Bruxelles · Chennai · Lausanne · New York · Oxford

Bibliographic information published by the Deutsche Nationalbibliothek.
The German National Library lists this publication in the German National Bibliography;
detailed bibliographic data is available on the Internet at http://dnb.d-nb.de.

Library of Congress Cataloging-in-Publication Data
Names: Karaosmanoğlu, Ali L. author
Title: Legal and military reforms : secularism and strategic thought from
   the empire to republican Turkey / Ali L. Karaosmanoğlu.
Description: New York : Peter Lang, 2025. | Includes bibliographical
   references and index.
Identifiers: LCCN 2025018507 | ISBN 9783631937082 hardback | ISBN
   9783631937099 ebook | ISBN 9783631937105 epub
Subjects: LCSH: Secularism--Turkey--History | Civil-military
   relations--Turkey--History | Law reform--Turkey--History |
   Turkey--History--Ottoman Empire, 1288-1918 | Turkey--History--20th
   century | Turkey--Foreign relations--Europe | Europe--Foreign
   relations--Turkey
Classification: LCC DR486 .K385 2025
LC record available at https://lccn.loc.gov/2025018507

ISBN 978-3-631-93708-2 (Print)
ISBN 978-3-631-93709-9 (ePDF)
ISBN 978-3-631-93710-5 (ePUB)
DOI 10.3726/b22860

© 2025 Peter Lang Group AG, Lausanne (Switzerland)
Published by Peter Lang GmbH, Berlin (Germany)

info@peterlang.com

This publication has been peer reviewed.

www.peterlang.com

To Nazlı, in celebration of 55 years of togetherness and love.

Contents

Acknowledgments

My academic journey began in Lausanne, Switzerland, where I obtained my Ph.D. in International Law. Therefore, I would first like to express my deepest gratitude to my advisor, Professor Georges Perrin, for his invaluable support and guidance throughout my thesis, which ultimately led to the publication of *Les Actions Militaires Coercitives et Non Coercitives des Nations Unies*. I am particularly grateful for his appreciation of my reference to Hans Kelsen, a distinguished scholar in law. Professor Georges Perrin kindly told me that he found my gesture "fully sensible," and his words of encouragement in this regard deeply touched me.

I never forgot to thank and praise Prof. Dr. İhsan Doğramacı and his son Prof. Ali Doğramacı. I always appreciated İhsan Hoca's establishment of quite a number of universities and research academies not only in Turkey, but also all over the World. They were the founders of Bilkent University in Ankara. Both Doğramacıs had been considerably successful in the establishment and direction of universities and research academies.

Together with a dear colleague of mine, Prof. Ersin Onulduran, we engaged in a dialogue with Seyfi Taşhan, who was a successful, reliable, and internationally respected businessman. Unlike international relations and foreign policy analysis, international law stands out as the only academic field where a significant dialogue has developed between scholars and foreign policy practitioners. The earliest efforts to bridge this gap emerged with the founding of the British Institute of International Affairs in 1926, later renamed *The Royal Institute of International Affairs (Chatham House)*. Among its members were prominent young scholars, including Arnold Toynbee. Despite receiving government funding, the institute operated as an independent center for research and publications. In Turkey, the first foreign policy think tank was established in 1974 by Seyfi Taşhan, who launched the initiative from his business office in Ankara. Taşhan started this initiative in 1971 with the publication of a quarterly policy-oriented journal, *"Foreign Policy—Dış Politika."* It is noteworthy that, in 2004, Seyfi Taşhan appointed a promising young professor at Bilkent University, Prof. Ersel Aydınlı. The best American universities and, think-thanks began to invite the leading Turkish university liberals and enlightened academics. Moreover, Prof. Aydınlı and I work together, helping one another.

In preparing this book, I would like to thank my assistants who emancipated my writings and provided support in research—Seyfi Bey's assistants and Eren Akpınar, a Ph.D. student in Istanbul University.

When Turkey aligned with NATO's identity and power politics after the Second World War, Ekavi Athanassopoulou became a considerable supporter of the Republican Turkey. Greece supported Turkey through naval power and land forces. Many other similar argumentations in British Universities began to attract more students. For instance, Philip Robins of Oxford University began to engage with the issues not only concerning Turkey but also Caucasus.

I would like to express my heartfelt gratitude to Tarık Oğuzlu for the enriching conversations and insightful discussions we shared during our lunch gatherings. I am also a close friend of Global Academia, founded by Mustafa Aydın and Mitat Çelikpala. Prof. Mustafa Aydın serves as its General Coordinator. I have always appreciated and supported their theoretical and political studies.

I would also like to mention two military strategic writers: Mesut Uyar has recently published a work on strategic maneuvers and training (Baskı, Ekim, 2021, İstanbul, Kronik Yayınları). Edward J. Erickson authored a military history and policy study, *Ottoman Army Effectiveness in World War I*, which is an excellent comparative study. I am grateful to both friends for their outstanding contributions to military studies.

I extend my genuine thanks to my daughter, Defne, for her invaluable assistance with organizing and editing the text. I am also deeply grateful to my son, Kerem, for his crucial contributions to the organization of the text and title, providing technical support, and offering his friendly help with repairs.

Introduction: Preliminary Thoughts and Historical Background

The title of the whole subject-matter is the theoretically tragic and strategic vision of politics. Moreover, the dialectical power of thinking and appropriate reasoning by the radical Enlightenment and Counter Enlightenment is without fighting or mutually offending each other. In Classical Greece, "Dialectic" meant the art of discussion or unification of contraries. Enlightenment and Counter Enlightenment can open empirical and experimental ways toward mutual arrangements. The dialectical power of thinking usually goes deeply into the subject-matter. It is also the basis of reciprocal, positive and international topical steps.

Nevertheless, in writing this book, I must certainly be a person who practices an unusual self-denial and devotion. The restraint would be kept under control or within limits: The mission characteristics of Armed Forces and Peace Operations, Military Tactics and Strategies, High-Tech and Low-tech, and many others, such as Cognitive Complexities. Moreover, they may be official, politically correct, and relevant militarily. At this point, I would like to begin the presentation of the preliminary thoughts and history.

If we do not want to give publicity to Islamic symbols and ideology, we should underline that the Islamic countries in the modern Middle East generally have two political tendencies. One is the Islamic fundamentalism in some countries as a reaction to their adoption of Western values and denying the Islamic ones. The second tendency is rejecting foreign political influence and hegemony, thereby giving special prominence to religious elements and nationalism. These two tendencies, which sometimes complement and sometimes conflict with each other, are present to varying degrees in all modern revolutionary and strategic movements. However, many Muslims and Westerners, as well as Western institutions, view secularizing socio-political life in Muslim states as unsuitable, believing it cannot produce meaningful results. This perception significantly shapes Muslim and Western views on intercultural relations and the development of world politics.[1]

According to Raymond Aron, interactions between states are shaped not only by power dynamics but also by the dialectic of ideas.[2] Henry A. Kissinger has a similar statement: "The deepest problems of equilibrium are not physical but psychological or moral. The shape of the future will depend ultimately on convictions which far transcend the physical balance of power." Then Kissinger poses two fundamental questions of multipolar worlds: How much diversity can we stand, and how much unity should we want? At first glance, these questions may sound ordinary and straightforward. However, they may not readily have a satisfactory final answer in heterogeneous societies.[3] When we encounter such paradoxical questions, we should consider historical and philosophical factors to deal with them.

The European state system, established by the Peace of Westphalia in 1648, forms the foundation of the Western understanding of modern international relations, often referred to as "classical statecraft." The 30 years' war, the final religious conflict of the Middle Ages, marked the end of the idea of a universal Christian community in international affairs and ushered in the secularization of political matters. Over time, this historical development has somewhat strengthened some of the national and inter-state solidarities.[4]

---

[1] Karaosmanoğlu, A. L. (1984). "Islam and Its Implications for the International System." In Metin Heper and Raphael Israeli (eds.), *Islam and Politics*, pp. 103–104. London: Croom Helm; repr., London and New York: Routledge, 2013.

[2] Aron, R. (1968). *Peace and War: A Theory of International Relations*. Translated by Richard Howard and Annette Baker Fox, p. 99. New York: Doubleday.

[3] Kissinger, H. A., (1974). *American Foreign Policy*, pp. 78–80. New York: W.W. Norto.

[4] Karaosmanoğlu, A. L. (1984). "Islam and Its Implications for the International System." In Metin Heper and Raphael Israeli (eds), *Islam and Politics*, p. 105, London: Croom Helm, repr., London and New York: Routledge, 2013; Morse, E. L. (1976). *Modernization and the Transformation of International Relations*, pp. 22–46, New York: The Free Press; and de Visscher, C. (1970). *Théories et réalités en droit international public* (4th edn.), pp. 11–18, Paris: Pedone. It should be noted, however, that the secularization of politics and the later rise of European liberalism did almost nothing to alter the inherited Western prejudice against the Ottoman Turks. Readers must not take this note as a

However, state sovereignty implied a distinction between domestic and international politics. Since foreign policy primarily focused on ensuring the survival of the sovereign state, it was generally regarded as more significant than domestic affairs. Political and ideological conflicts make it difficult to define political and national allegiances, blurring the boundary between domestic and international affairs.[5] Edmund Burke illustrated the consequences of this paradoxical system during the French Revolution:

> I never thought we could make peace with the system; because it was not for the sake of an object we pursued in rivalry with each other; but with the system itself that we were at war. As I understood the matter, we were at war not with its conduct but its existence; convinced that its existence and its hostility were the same.[6]

Some preliminary thoughts concerning the connection between ideology—often expressed through religion—and political action have been a longstanding aspect of international relations history. For approximately 13 centuries, throughout the Middle Ages and modern periods, Islam and Christianity remained in constant conflict. This struggle involved two competing and at times hostile, religious, cultural, and political systems, each believing in its mission and message for humanity. Furthermore, both were convinced that eliminating the other was essential for the greater good of society. At the same time, however, they had "peaceful coexistence." Interestingly, in the thirteenth and fourteenth centuries, there were "cold wars" called *guerra fría*.[7] Such brief periods prepared the ground for the limited exchange of civilian values, including secularism. Ideological conflict, whether through warfare, proselytism, or subversion, persisted into modern times. This was

---

reproach. We all know that, despite some intellectual and scientific studies in both parties, mutual prejudices have continued for a long time, and they are still on.

[5] Karaosmanoğlu, A. L. (1984). "Islam and Its Implications for the International System." In Metin Heper and Raphael Israeli (eds), *Islam and Politics*. London: Croom Helm, repr., London and New York: Routledge, 2013.

[6] Burke, E. (1826). *Works* (London), (vol. VIII), pp. 214–215; Karaosmanoğlu, A. L. (1984). "Islam and Its Implications for the International System." In Metin Heper and Raphael Israeli (eds), *Islam and Politics*, p. 105. London: Croom Helm, repr., London and New York: Routledge, 2013.

[7] von Grunebaum, G. E. (1953). *Medieval Islam: A Study in Cultural Orientation* (2nd ed). Chicago: University of Chicago Press, pp. 1–10; and Khadduri, M. (1966) *Introduction to the Islamic Law of Nations: Shaybani's Siyar*, p. 22. Baltimore: Johns Hopkins Press.

evident when the Ottoman Empire expanded the Islamic order into Central Europe's vulnerable regions, only to be eventually dismantled by continuous European assaults and the rise of nationalism. Although the world orders shaped by the two rival religions were initially rigid and exclusive, both adapted to their surroundings by embracing a more pragmatic approach. This shift was marked by accepting reciprocity, leading to broader mutual recognition.[8]

Classical Muslim doctrine categorized the world into *dar al-Islam* (Pax Islamica) and *dar al-harb* (the abode of war). *Dar al-Islam* included both Islamic and non-Islamic communities that accepted Muslim rule, whereas *dar al-harb* encompassed all other regions and groups. This division was considered valid until the complete and defensive subjugation of the abode of war. This strongly divisive principle has refrained from absolutism by leaving some diplomatically and politically important gates open to secularism. The Treaty of Karlowitz in 1699 marked a significant shift in the military balance between Christian Europe and the Ottoman Empire. From then on, the Ottoman state employed balance-of-power diplomacy not to expand westward but to slow its retreat eastward. This policy was supported by European powers, which sought to prevent a sudden collapse of the Ottoman Empire, fearing it would create a dangerous power vacuum in the East.

Halil İnalcık puts forward a view in an argument:

> Within the Islamic community of peoples, Turks have had a special state tradition from the time they entered and controlled the Islamic world in the eleventh century. Originated in the steppe empires, this tradition can be defined as recognition of the state's absolute independence of action and upholding the state's absolute right to legislate on public matters. Thus, in Turkish states, a body of laws and regulations existed independently from the Islamic law, and led public life in the highest interests of the state and community, giving elasticity in formulating state policies.[9]

---

[8] Majid Khadduri, (1965) "The Islamic Theory of International Relations and Its Contemporary Relevance." In J. Harris Proctor (ed), *Islam and International Relations*, p. 31. New York: Praeger; Bozeman, A. B. (1971). *The Future of Law in a Multicultural World*, pp. 82–84. Princeton: Princeton University Press.

[9] İnalcık, H. (July 1980) "Turkey between Europe and the Middle East," *Foreign Policy*, VIII(3–4), 7. For more details, see İnalcık, H. (2011). *Rönesans Avrupası: Türkiye'nin Batı Medeniyetiyle Özdeşleşme Süreci*. İstanbul: İş Bankası Kültür Yayınları; and İnalcık, H. (2016). *Osmanlı Tarihinde İslamiyet ve Devlet*, İstanbul: İş Bankası Kültür Yayınları.

This Turkish tradition of relations with Western European states and Russia added new and different cultural qualities to the Ottoman elites. This began to produce, in the early eighteenth century, a more moderating and secularizing effect on nationalism and domestic life. Since then, this development has been a serious, unsolved internal and international issue not only in Turkey but all over the whole world.

At this point, I wish to go back and refer to an argumentative opinion about the strong dichotomy between *Dar al-Harp* and *Dar al-Islam*. The historical record does not confirm such a picture of the possibility of permanent wars between the Ottomans and European states. Thereby again, it was not impossible to return mutually to the "otherizational" treatments against each other. There was always a religious conservatism between Christian Europe and the Ottoman Turks; however, in the Ottoman state, religious conservatism was neither an absolute nor unchangeable principle. For instance, the Ottoman state did not formally exchange resident ambassadors until the eighteenth century. As a matter of fact, this was not a real delay. Despite conservatism, considerable diplomatic, economic, and military interactions existed between the Ottoman imperial system and the European states. Sultan Bayezid (1481–1512), a pious ruler, did not hesitate to make a political agreement with the Pope. Another well-known example was Sultan Süleyman's (Kanuni, 1520–1566) military alliance with the King of France (François I) against the Habsburgs' aggressions against France.[10]

This book explores the historical, philosophical, and strategic dimensions of Turkey's legal and military reforms, with a particular emphasis on secularism, military strategy, and the impact of Western thought on Turkish modernization. Through a structured analysis, spanning different historical

---

Additionally, see Mantran, R. (1989). *Histoire de l'Empire Ottoman*, pp. 103–109. Paris: Fayard.

[10] Yurdusev, Y. (2004) "The Ottoman Attitude toward Diplomacy." In Yurdusev N. (ed.), *Ottoman Diplomacy: Conventional or Unconventional*, pp. 5–30. London: Palgrave Macmillan. For more details, see additional articles by other writers in the same volume edited by Yurdusev.

periods, I examine how these reforms have shaped the country's legal traditions, state institutions, and strategic positioning.

The first section, *The Pre-Modern Era*, investigates the legal and administrative foundations of the Ottoman Empire, focusing on the coexistence of Sultanic Law (*Kanun*) and Religious Law (*Şeriat*). It considers how these dual legal structures influenced governance and statecraft. The following section, *The Modern Era*, traces the transition from the Ottoman Empire to the Republic of Turkey, emphasizing the evolution of the state tradition, military transformations, and the intellectual trajectory of Mustafa Kemal Atatürk. The final historical section, *The Cold War and Post-Cold War Era*, explores Turkey's integration into NATO, its approach to nuclear strategy, and the evolving dynamics of civil-military relations in the context of democratization. Beyond these historical discussions, a dedicated chapter on *Historical and Philosophical Considerations* examines the role of hermeneutics, the ideas of Charles Taylor and Richard Lebow, and international relation theories in shaping debates on secularism in Turkey. The book concludes with a reflection on the enduring intellectual and strategic tensions between the Enlightenment and Counter-Enlightenment, particularly, in relation to military theory and political philosophy.

To conclude, I move beyond institutional and strategic analyses to reconsider Turkey's place in European and global history. I challenge the idea that the Ottoman Empire and modern Turkey were separate from Europe, arguing instead that the Ottomans actively shaped the continent's intellectual, legal, and military traditions. By rejecting rigid dichotomies, I offer a more integrated perspective on Turkey's historical and geopolitical positioning.

Legal and military reforms in both the Ottoman and early Republican periods were not isolated shifts but part of a broader exchange with European thought and strategy. These transformations were shaped by—and, in turn, helped shape—European intellectual and strategic traditions. Rather than reinforcing an East-West divide, I highlight the profound interconnections that have long defined Turkey's legal and military identity.

Pre-Modern Era

2.1. Sultanic Law (Kanun) and Religious Law (Şeriat)

After the conquest of Constantinople, Sultan Mehmet, the Conqueror divided, without delay, the legal system of the Ottoman Empire into two sub-systems. Many jurists maintained that Sultanic law was both necessary and valid, as the *şeriat* provided no guidance on the matter. They argued that the Sultan's laws were based on widely accepted customs or principles through analogy, served the well-being of the Islamic community, could be effectively enforced by the sovereign, and did not conflict with the *şeriat*. According to Tursun Bey, the legal adviser of the Sultan, Sultans must have the authority to make regulations and enact laws entirely on their initiative. These laws, separate from the *şeriat* and referred to as *kanun*, were grounded in rational rather than religious principles and were primarily applied in public and administrative law. These legal regulations were considered essential for prosperity, success in international relations, and the regulation of the people's interests.

With the spread of Turkish rule, the Ottoman legal system became firmly established in Islamic legal practice, customs, and ethics. Furthermore, rulers were unwilling to acknowledge any restrictions on their power. Ottoman *kanun* originated as *fermans*, meaning sultanic decrees (Sultan's law), which the Sultans issued as conditions required.

Kanun was classified into three categories. The first included decrees resembling laws that sultans issued on specific matters. The second consisted of decrees addressing particular regions or social groups. The third comprised general *kanunnames* that applied to the entire Empire. Mehmet the Conqueror issued quite a number of legislative decrees in order to solve critical legal issues. Their preface attributed the codification of *kanunnames* to Kanuni Sultan Suleyman the Magnificent (1520–1566)—the criminal code applied throughout the Empire, serving as a *kanun* code that supplemented the şeriat. For severe crimes, such as murder, rape, and robbery with violence, it stated officially that execution or mutilation had to be carried out. For many other legal violations, there were fixed monetary fines. These clarifications (*lex talionis*) were also adopted by şeriat law. Adulterers were punished according to their means: the rich, the middle-income group, and the poor. For illegal sexual relations, there were fines based on the offender's means. The severity of the punishment depended on factors such as the individual's gender, status (free or slave), marital status, and religion (Muslim or non-Muslim). The second member of each pair paid half the fine.[11]

2.2. Provincial and Provisional Administrations

During the conquest, the Ottoman administration in European territories was gradually established. Regions directly controlled by the Ottomans were organized as *sanjaks* and separated from areas designated for Holy War by a buffer zone, which could be a frontier region or a vassal state. In these vassal states, the Ottomans occasionally allowed ruling dynasties autonomy in domestic affairs while requiring them to pay an annual tribute and provide military support. Some areas were maintained as frontier *beyliks* or vassal principalities. During the fifteenth and sixteenth centuries, newly conquered territories were typically placed under the direct rule of *sanjak beyis*, who were later overseen by a *beylerbeyi*. For example, in 1533, the *beylerbeyilik* of Algiers was established and granted to Hayreddin Barbarossa to unify Ottoman naval forces against the fleet and corsairs of the Holy Roman Empire (Habsburgs). Moreover, Barbarossa was appointed as the navy admiral (*kapudan-i derya*)

---

[11] İnalcık, H. (1973). *The Ottoman Empire: The Classical Age (1300–1600)*. Translated by N. Itzkowitz, and C. Imber, pp. 70–75. London: Weidenfeld and Nicolson; and İnalcık, H. (2016). *Osmanlı Tarihinde İslamiyet ve Devlet*, pp. 57–84. İstanbul: İş Bankası Kültür Yayınları.

of the Ottoman Empire. He had conquered numerous ports and islands in the Mediterranean even before his assignment.

After 1590, the *beylerbeyiliks*, which were later referred to as *eyalets*, were reduced in size. Towards the year 1610, they increased to 32 *eyalets* in the Empire. The government could enforce the *timar* system only in regions where the *sanjak* system, Ottoman law, and Ottoman administration were well-established. The *timar* system was not in force in some of the Arab countries; thus, some local autonomy was maintained. However, the Sultan stationed Janissary garrisons in each province and appointed a governor, *defterdar*, and *kadı*, collectively known as *salyane*. Unlike the *timar* system, the provincial revenues were not distributed to *sipahis*. Instead, after covering all military and administrative expenses, the governor was required to send a fixed annual sum, called *salyane*, to the capital. These provinces came to be known as *salyane provinces*. Consequently, several regions retained a degree of autonomy, including the Christian vassal principalities of Moldavia, Wallachia, Transylvania, Bosnia-Herzegovina, Kosovo, Albania, Dubrovnik, Georgia, Circassia, and, in the seventeenth century, the rebellious Cossack leaders. The Muslim principalities, such as the Khanate of Crimea, the Sherifate of Mecca, and, for a time, Tripoli, Tunisia, and Algeria, also maintained their status as frontier provinces. In the sixteenth century, the Ottoman government asserted theoretical sovereignty over Venice, Poland, and the Habsburg Empire—all tribute-paying states—and over France when Francis I sought Ottoman assistance, leading to an alliance that allowed Barbarossa to use French harbors and seaports.[12]

The beys on the frontier operated independently from the central government. Some Sultans and their advisers disdained such a semi-federal system, regarding it as shameful. Interestingly, Sultan Mehmet, the Conqueror, was a radical centralizer. When he came to the throne, he did not delay formulating plans to obliterate them or, at least, decrease their large number. The Sultan also decided to limit their autonomy further while simultaneously strengthening the Janissary Corps stationed in the territories of the semi-federated provincial administrations. The Application of these reforms would take a very long and exhausting time, complicating the central government's

---

12 İnalcık, H. (1973). *The Ottoman Empire: The Classical Age (1300–1600)*. Translated by N. Itzkowitz, and C. Imber, pp. 104–118. London: Weidenfeld and Nicolson.

international and religious affairs. The Empire did not need such a reformation. It accepted members of the equivalent caste from newly conquered
states as part of the military class, allowing Christian fief-holders to become
timar-holding *sipahis*. Some of these fief-holders, along with their sons, con-
verted to Islam. In the fifteenth and sixteenth centuries, a large portion of
the *timar*-holding cavalry, like the Janissary Corps, was composed of slaves.[13]

Kemal H. Karpat asserts a slightly different but interesting approach to
the historical issues surrounding autonomous provisional administrations:

> For instance, there are, in Ottoman history, periods of religious reaction, liberalism,
> and reformism. Actually, all these religious movements and attitudes were condi-
> tioned by social changes and by the specific actions of certain social groups that
> had a powerful interest in liberal, conservative, or even heretical interpretations
> of Islam. The key feature in these various interpretations was not the theological
> substance of Islam but certain aspects of the social system.[14]

During the early years of the Ottoman state, as institutions were established
and developed, a liberal religious approach dominated, best represented by
the concept of "frontier Islam." However, after the Ottoman central statecraft
had learned and developed its basic social and political constitution and a
separate political legal system outside the religious one, Mehmet II (1451–1481)
consolidated its power, largely due to the Janissaries. The Islamic religious system became conservative, even reactionary, during the rule of Sultan Beyazit
II (1481–1512). Although the Janissaries were unorthodox and participated
in the Bektashi *tariqat*, and while some of them probably carried some relics
of the Christian and European culture, they never hesitated to fight against
the religious and irreligious groups revolting against the central government.

After the period of the Uç Beyleri (the Frontier Lords) (1299–1402), the
chief characteristic of the Ottoman state, became a continuous effort by its
central administration to consolidate power through economic, social, and
political reorganization of the system (1421–1596). The roles of the throne
and the dynasty within the socio-political structure were clearly defined

---

[13] İnalcık, H. (1973). *The Ottoman Empire: The Classical Age (1300–1600)*. Translated by
N. Itzkowitz, and C. Imber, pp. 104–118. London: Weidenfeld and Nicolson.

[14] Karpat, K. H. (1974). "The Stages of Ottoman History." In K. H. Karpat (ed.), *The
Ottoman State and Its Place in World History*, pp. 79–98. Leiden: E.J. Brill.

through succession laws and a favorable interpretation of the dynasty's origins, connecting it to the great Muslim rulers of the past. The central army, particularly the Janissaries, became a key military force and served as the means through which the central government's authority was extended into the provinces. At the same time, the economy and foreign trade were tightly regulated by the government, putting aside the Venetians as key merchants and opening commercial opportunities to native commercial groups. However, this development was far from ameliorating the economic conflict between Ottomans and Venetians in the Eastern Mediterranean. Sultan Mehmet, the Conqueror, introduced the basic political, social, and administrative rules that remained the official foundation of the Ottoman state nearly until its end. It emphasized the supremacy of the central government, signifying that political authority gradually took precedence over all private and voluntary organizations, as well as culture and religion. This was a statist system centered around a bureaucracy that the Sultan sought to shield from external influences, employing every measure to ensure its unwavering loyalty to the state. The bureaucracy ultimately became a distinct social class. Most of them were the *kul* (slaves) of the Sultan. Their main purpose was to protect the Empire's economic, financial, and social foundations. Their rising integrity and power created considerable reaction among the old established provincial elites. Some scholars mentioned that this struggle was between converts and old-time Muslims. Kemal Karpat corrected this argument. Actually, it was a power struggle between the elites of the *kul* and the older provincial elites. At the end of this paragraph, I wish to emphasize that it is irrelevant to argue about the effect of Mehmet the Conqueror's reforms on provincial autonomies, as under changing circumstances, some of the *Ayans* benefited from the opportunity to increase their autonomies. The provincial autonomy system remained and worked until the end of the Ottoman state.[15] Economic and cultural exchanges between the Ottoman Muslim East and Christian Europe were common and became an integral part of daily life.

---

[15] Karpat, K. H. (1974). "The Stages of Ottoman History." In K. H. Karpat (ed.), *The Ottoman State and Its Place in World History*, pp. 79–98. Leiden: E.J. Brill; İnalcık, H. (1996)."The Meaning of Legacy: The Ottoman Case." In L. Carl Brown (ed.), *Imperial Legacy*, pp. 24–28. New York: Columbia University Press.

Modern Era

3.1. The State Tradition and the Ottoman Legacy

Understanding the close connection between Islam and nationalism is essential for grasping the processes of both separation and unity in the Middle East. In this region, religion and nationalism are both in conflict and deeply intertwined. Although distinct political entities and nation-states have existed within the Islamic world, Islamic law does not acknowledge clear, permanent divisions within the *umma Muhammadiyya*. As a result, nationalist movements in the Middle East function within a framework of religious and cultural radical nationalism, often carrying an underlying pan-Islamic element that emerges in times of crisis. Von Grunebaum highlights this dual nature of Middle Eastern nationalism:

> On the one hand, it presents itself as a nationalistic movement of the conventional European style, based on a sense of racial kinship and with certain geographical claims that are justified on historical grounds. On the other hand, it is a thinly disguised Mahdist movement aiming at a forcible purification of Islam and the revival of the traditionally demanded imperialism of the *umma*. The interlocking of these two activist drives gives Arab nationalism its strength and makes it proof against the hesitations of a purely secular, real-political movement.[16]

The relationship between religion and nationalism adds an inherent instability to the Middle Eastern system. The absence of *realpolitik* is reflected

---

[16] von Grunebaum, G. E. (1953). *Medieval Islam: A Study in Cultural Orientation* (2nd edn.), p. 224. Chicago: University of Chicago Press. See also Karaosmanoğlu, A. L.

in the revolutionary policies in countries like Nasser's Egypt, Khaddafi's Libya, and Khomeini's Iran. These leaders prioritize creating a new reality over manipulating the existing one. They reject gradualism and compromise with circumstances, believing that "truth" or "what is right" cannot be negotiated. As a result, they use traditional diplomatic methods primarily as propaganda to demoralize opponents rather than seeking conflict resolution.[17] This approach, found not only in fundamentalist regimes but also in some modernist states and groups, sets Middle Eastern statecraft apart from the more secular Western world.

Religious and sectarian differences contribute to instability in the region despite its cultural homogeneity, especially in the Arab world. Christian minorities, like the Copts in Egypt and the Maronites in Lebanon, coexist with various forms of Islam that are sometimes linked to states and other times to specific communities within the same state. Shi'ism is associated with Iran, and in Iraq, a Sunni minority governs a large Shi'i population. Religious and sectarian tensions are exacerbated by social inequalities and militant ideologies calling for revolutionary change. The situation is further complicated by regional and global powers seeking to expand their influence. Another significant issue for the Arabs is the unresolved Palestinian question, which remains a symbol of legitimacy for Arab governments. As a result, legitimacy in domestic politics is closely tied to foreign policy actions.

While Muslim nationalism opposes both Marxist-Leninist atheism and Western "materialism," its primary emphasis is on anti-Western sentiment. This hostility is rooted in historical and political factors. First, it stems from the longstanding conflict between Islam and Christendom since the Middle Ages. Second, during the nineteenth century, Western powers increased their control over Islamic lands. Third, many Arabs and non-Arab Muslims view Zionism as a form of Western imperialism and Israel as an extension of the West, particularly the United States, in the Middle East.[18] This creates

---

(1984). "Islam and Its Implications for the International System." In M. Heper, and R. Israeli (eds.) (2013). *Islam and Politics*, p. 111. London: Croom Helm, repr., London and New York: Routledge.

[17] See this type of political behavior discussed in a critical chapter by Kissinger, H. A. (1974). *American Foreign Policy*, pp. 46–48. New York: W.W. Norton.

[18] Sayegh, F. A. (1966). *The Zionist Diplomacy*, p. 143. Beirut.

a significant moral and geographical disadvantage for the West, especially the USA, in maintaining its influence in a strategically important region.

In the modern international system, which was once shaped by the Christian-Muslim divide, Islam is neither completely irrelevant nor an inflexible determining factor. After a long history of competition and rivalry, both sides have learned to separate ideology from the practice of foreign relations.[19] Today, there is no distinct Islamic perspective on world order that influences foreign policy, nor is there a Muslim approach to international politics that contrasts with the Western one. Islam does not set forth any transcendent foreign policy goals. Instead, it functions as a symbol of legitimacy, representing the value system based on the political regime's legitimacy. In this context, Islam, as a transnational cultural force, links domestic legitimacy with international politics, blurring the distinction between the temporal and the spiritual, as well as between the domestic and the international.[20]

L. Carl Brown of Princeton University edited an excellent history book titled *The Ottoman Empire's Legacy on the Balkans and the Middle East.*[21] The book contains articles and essays written by the master scholars of Christianity and Islam. However, to prepare ourselves for studying the alternative roads of a rising republic, we have to begin by examining the essential characteristics of the Republic in question—namely, the Republic established by Mustafa Kemal Atatürk and his companions on October 29, 1923. If we want to understand Atatürk's policies and political actions profoundly, we should read scholarly works instead of following legendary tales. An essential article to read would undoubtedly be Ergun Özbudun's

---

[19] Majid Khadduri, (1963) "The Islamic System: Its Competition and Coexistence with Western Systems." In R. H. Nolte (ed.), *The Modern Middle East*, p. 155. New York: Atheneum.

[20] Karaosmanoğlu, A. L. (1984). "Islam and Its Implications for the International System." In M. Heper, and R. Israeli (eds), *Islam and Politics*. London: Croom Helm, pp. 114–116; repr., London and New York: Routledge, 2013.

[21] L. Carl Brown (ed.) (1996). *Imperial Legacy: The Ottoman Imprint on the Balkans and the Middle East*. New York: Columbia University Press.

publication in Carl Brown's edited *Imperial Legacy*.[22] Özbudun begins his article with the following words:

> One of the important legacies of the Ottoman Empire is state tradition. By this, I mean a strong and centralized state, reasonably effective by the standards of its day, highly autonomous of social forces, and occupying a central and highly valued place in Ottoman political culture. This tradition, we argue, continues to affect politics in Turkey and in other successor states, albeit in modified form. The first section elucidates the key concepts related to state autonomy and state capabilities. In the second section, the politico-cultural conditions that created a distinctive Ottoman state tradition are briefly set out. The third section discusses specifics resulting from the Ottoman state tradition and shared by the contemporary successor states. In the fourth and fifth sections, respectively, two dimensions of state strength—autonomy and capabilities—are discussed with reference to the successor states, with particular emphasis on Turkey, Egypt, Syria, and Iraq. In the concluding section, prospects for the development of democratic (*my adding* * *republican**) governments in the region are examined.

Beyond these topics, we have been particularly interested in studying the Ottoman impact on the trajectories of republican developments in Turkey. The most significant political legacy of the Ottoman Empire to its successor states was sovereignty or, at least, autonomy. Turkey gained sovereignty after winning the War of Independence against the European invading powers (1919–1922). The autonomous successor states retained their traditions in the Balkans and the Middle East. At this point, I would like to remind you again of the significant and unchangeable characteristics of the Ottoman Empire. Briefly, it was anything but a nation-state. It was a multi-national, multi-ethnic, multi-religious, and multi-sectarian state. However, most Arab states have refused Ottoman pluralism due to the combination of their radical nationalism and Islam. Egypt held a middle position, leaning more towards Turkey. While Turkish nationalism emerged relatively late, the Young Turks

---

[22] Özbudun, E. (1996). "The Continuing Ottoman Legacy and the State Tradition in the Middle East." In L. C. Brown (ed.), *Imperial Legacy: The Ottoman Imprint on the Balkans and the Middle East*, pp. 133–157. New York: Columbia University Press.

and later the Kemalists succeeded in creating a new collective identity centered around Turkish nationalism, replacing the Ottoman-Islamic identity.[23]

At this point, I do not want to stop this chapter, enriched by Ergun Özbudun's arguments, which carefully avoid cognitive dissonance. The most significant political legacy of the Ottoman Empire to its successor states is state autonomy. A mix of political, social, economic, cultural, and historical factors has fostered this region's strong and independent state tradition. Since gaining independence, nearly all successor states have maintained this tradition and, in some cases, have even reinforced it, particularly through oil revenues and the expansion of bureaucratic structures and new technology devices, which are highly profitable to their owners but harmful to small-scale trailers. Another important countertrend was the rise of Islamic groups. In 1996 (the date of Carl Brown's publication), it was probably too early for a significant transformation in the Middle East.

Nevertheless, despite conflicting trends, the Ottoman administrative legacy remains alive in the modern Middle East. In Carl Brown's same publication, Carter Vaughn Findley identifies key themes of the Ottoman administrative legacy and argues their saliency for studying government and administration today. Surveying the history of politics and administration over the last centuries, Findley puts forward six themes of the Ottoman legacy that still seem important for the region: centralization and the reassertion of state authority; indigenous versus imported ideologies; elite formation and inter-elite competition; institutional expansion; mass mobilization; and the state's role in the economy.[24]

3.2. Strategy from Clausewitz to Atatürk

There is no evidence that Mustafa Kemal Atatürk read Clausewitz. However, in the conduct of the War of Independence, we see that many practices that

---

[23] Özbudun, E. (1996). "The Continuing Ottoman Legacy and the State Tradition in the Middle East." In L. C. Brown (ed.), *Imperial Legacy: The Ottoman Imprint on the Balkans and the Middle East*, pp. 136–138, 153. New York: Columbia University Press.

[24] Findley, C. V. (1996). "The Ottoman Administrative Legacy and the Modern Middle East." In L. Carl Brown (ed.), *Imperial Legacy: The Ottoman Imprint on the Balkans and the Middle East*, p. 158. New York: Columbia University Press.

brought Mustafa Kemal Pasha closer to Clausewitz were successfully implemented: the integration of military force with politics and diplomacy, the highly organized retreat to Sakarya after the defeat in the West (Kütahya-Eskişehir); the withdrawal of enemy forces into the interior of Anatolia; and the statement, "There is no line defense, there is surface defense. That line is the whole homeland"; integrating offense and defense; integrating tactical, operative, and strategic levels; combining material power and spiritual values; integrating genius and long-term planning (building a new state) with individual and current thinking; integrating merit with social will and sentiment; pursuing fleeing enemy soldiers beyond the borders of the country after winning the field battles; knowing how to stop when the political purpose of the war is realized; and considering uprisings against the Kuvay-i Milliye as a part of the War of Independence, using irregular forces to suppress them. All these practices are antinomies (paradoxes) unique to our War of Independence. These are not tactical or strategic principles or maxims that Clausewitz intended to be applied to win a war. Clausewitz was never in favor of a good commander, putting the general rules learned in military education and training in his pocket and taking them to the battlefield. Especially if the commander or commander-in-chief was a "genius" beyond good, he should set the rules according to the conditions on the battlefield, in the country, and abroad. Mustafa Kemal Pasha had already done this. Clausewitz did not lay down principles that must be followed for success in war, especially at the strategic level. Instead, he developed an open-ended method to better perceive the current situation and predict the future.

Generally and unequivocally, until Republican Turkey became a member of NATO, the Prussian-German influence on security matters continued. This was a simple militaristic rather than a Republican intellectual and academic influence. The concept of strategy was developed within the framework of "national security" and expanded to include economic issues. This conceptual transformation began with the adoption of the idea of "Total War," introduced by General Erich von Ludendorf. Until the end of the Second World War, Turkey always felt at risk of war and insecurity. It would most likely be a total war if it had to fight a war. In other words, the country would be at war not only with its army but also with its entire economy, resources, and society. Until the end of the Cold War, Turkey's understanding of national security was dominated by such a strategy. As has been repeatedly pointed out, there is no similarity or equivalence between total war and Clausewitz's concept of absolute war.

Total war is a military doctrine or strategic choice, while absolute war is a methodological, rational, and hypothetical model used to understand and explain the nature of war. Warring parties tend to escalate violence against each other; if one side increases violence, the other responds in kind. This movement of reciprocity continues, escalating the violence upward until it reaches an "absolute." The result is, of course, catastrophe. However, in "real war," the "fog of war"—that is, the unknowns of war—and "friction"—the material and immaterial factors that impede the movements of war—intervene as factors that stifle escalation. Another important obstacle in a real war is the political aims and political relationships of the warring parties. It is important to remember, however, that politics cannot only limit the escalation of violence but also stimulate it.[25]

3.3. Restructuring the State and Society in the Late Ottoman Empire

Most well-known books about the rise of the Republic of Turkey were written and published in the new millennium, after 2000 or at least in the 1990s. These intellectual and academic writers have generally favored republican forms of government. Consequently, they prefer to begin with the history of the late Ottoman Empire as, for example, about the Tanzimat, the Young Turks' movements, and the Hamidian Regime. M. Şükrü Hanioğlu of Princeton University has been an important, exceptional scholar who has never forgotten the early secularist Sultans of the fifteenth and the sixteenth centuries and their political and legitimate power to accomplish the combination of governmental centralism with provincial administrative autonomy. Nevertheless, we have already addressed the legal reforms

---

[25] Karaosmanoğlu, A. L. (2011) "Yirminci Yüzyılda Savaşı Tartışmak: Clausewitz Yeniden," *Uluslararası İlişkiler* 8 (29), 5–25; Strachan, H. (2007) "Clausewitz and the Dialectics of War." In H. Strachan, and A. Herberg-Rothe (eds.), *Clausewitz in the Twenty-First Century*, Oxford: Oxford University Press; Brodie, B. (1973) *War and Politics*, pp. 8–47, 90, 262, 444–453, 493. London: Cassell.

of the early Ottoman Empire. Thus, we could directly pass on to the late Ottoman Empire and Republican Turkey.

Şükrü Hanioğlu begins his analysis by emphasizing the challenges of covering nearly 150 years of significant change across a vast geographic area. He notes the need to contextualize events from 1798 to 1918 by looking at the late eighteenth-century Ottoman Empire and the legacy it left to the successor states. Hanioğlu critiques the widespread nationalist narratives that present Ottoman history as a linear path toward inevitable collapse, leading to modern nation-states like Turkey. This teleological perspective, he argues, distorts historical processes by forcing them into a predetermined narrative of decline and Westernization. A central aim of his work is to move beyond these assumptions to provide a clearer understanding of the period on its own terms:

> The point is not to deny the significance of the link between the successor nation-states (especially Turkey) and their Ottoman past... But the attempt to frame late Ottoman history in a narrative of imperial collapse to the relentless drumbeat of the march of progress usually associated with Westernization, nationalism, and secularization, prevents a clear understanding of the developments in question. Rectifying this error is a major goal of this book.[26]

I would like to underline an important characteristic of Hanioğlu's books. Each book should not limit itself to single events. His explanations should emphasize historical trends and processes as integrating Ottoman history into world history and taking each of them, in turn, and to the future. Most problems arising from Western modernity were not completely unknown to the Ottoman Empire. They addressed secularization, reconciling religion with scientific progress, challenging traditional societal foundations, reacting to public opinion, integrating technology into administration, managing urbanization, and reflecting cultural transformation (Westernization). The late Ottoman Empire had a dynamic relationship with the Great Powers of Europe. This book provides a detailed analysis of the late Ottoman Empire in the nineteenth century and the challenge of modernity. Readers also have the opportunity to explore the Tanzimat era, the Hamidian regime, the

---

[26] M. Şükrü Hanioğlu (2008). *A Brief History of the Late Ottoman Empire*, pp. 1–5. Princeton: Princeton University Press.

Young Turk Revolution, military weakness, military reforms, and victories. These events and their process through unification opened all the gates to the republican future of Turkey without delay. Before starting to put forward my ideas on the construction of the Turkish Republic and Kemalism, I wish to conclude this argument with a sentence from Hanioğlu: "The Ottoman experience provides a superb opportunity to examine the impact of modernity in a non-European setting. This brief account of this impact will have accomplished its goal if it succeeds in inspiring a new generation of scholars to take this endeavor further."[27]

During the political reforms made in the Ottoman state (1839–1876), the Grand Vezir said, "We have abolished the legal differences between Christians and Muslims; they are now all Ottomans and equal." the British ambassador asked, "This means that, from now on, Muslim women will be able to marry Christians." and the Grand Vezir shouted, "No... That will not do!" and he jumped up from his seat. It cannot be denied that great things were achieved in Tanzimat. The palace, the Bab-ı Âli, and the vigilant Ottomans agreed that we would become Europeans or the seven-clawed imperialist giant *Düvel-i Muazzama* (Great Powers) would tear us apart and turn us back into Asian herds. The Tanzimatists showed great courage to save the Ottoman Turks from this dark fate. At the beginning of the nineteenth century, it was more difficult to say that Christians and Muslims were equal in law than changing the Arabic script to Latin script in 1928. But the *medrese* (religious schools) next to the modern schools; the *sharia* next to the new laws; the *sharia* courts next to the civil courts; the *qadi* next to the judge; the *mufti* next to the governor; and the *sheikhulislâm* next to the grand vezir, remained as they were even in 1920. The sultan himself was also the caliph. Towards the 100th anniversary of the Tanzimat, we were in the twentieth century at Bab-ı Âli and in the seventh century at Süleymaniye. Not only the family, with all its rights, but even contemplation at the university was under the control of the *Sharia*. However, in the Faculty of Literature, students used to read philosophy rooted in a religious *medrese* tradition.[28]

---

[27] Hanioğlu, M. S. (2008). *A Brief History of the Late Ottoman Empire*, pp. 6–212. Princeton: Princeton University Press.
[28] Hanioğlu, M. S. (2008). *A Brief History of the Late Ottoman Empire*, pp. 6–212. Princeton: Princeton University Press.

3.3.1. Secular reforms in Republican Turkey

The pressure of a medieval theocracy was felt in three-quarters of the country. The article stating that the laws to be enacted by the Grand National Assembly would not be contrary to the provisions of the *sharia* had not been removed from the main provisions of the Constitutional Law. In the founding period of the Republic, the decisive victory in the civilizational struggle that had been going on for a century was won with the Civil Code and laicism. The passing of the Civil Code by the Grand National Assembly and the purification of the Constitution according to the principles of laicism—by removing the article that the religion of the state is Islam—was the coronation ceremony of our revolutionary cause. There was no longer any obstacle for the Turkish nation to evolve into a twentieth-century society. Beyond that was the question of education.

For a century, reactionaries have been claiming that Westernization means leaving religion and nationality. Kemalism put an end to this fairy tale. For the first time, we were also regaining our Turkishness. Our borders in Europe and Asia, between the two countries, became what is called National Unity and were first realized in Revolutionary Turkey. As Falih Rıfkı Atay states, in Tanzimat literature, there were one or two intellectuals who said, "I am a Turk?" They will erect a statue of him. In Revolutionary Turkey, there is no longer an intellectual who does not say, "I am a Turk."[29]

Atay asserts that in Western civilization, the Italians would be Italian, the Germans would be German, and the Turks would be Turkish. In the Islamic Orient, the Arab was Arab, the Persian was Persian, and even the Albanian was Albanian, but the Turk was not Turkish. In Atay's words, as early as 1915, when he was a university professor, the philosopher Naim Hoxha found the only salvation for Turkishness was its Arabization. Its language had to be Arabic. Falih Rıfkı Atay remembers an Eskisehir deputy, a *hodja* in the Second National Assembly, who was always careful to pronounce the word "and" in the Arabic dialect. Most of the icazet certificates of *medrese* and *tekke* elders had a lineage ending with a Companion, especially Abu Bakr.[30]

Westernization also meant getting rid of Arabization and Turkization. Religion is a matter of conscience. Islam is the yeast of nationality in the

---

[29] Atay, F. R. (1999). *Çankaya*, Çağdaş Matbaacılık ve Yayıncılık.
[30] Atay, F. R. (1999). *Çankaya*, Çağdaş Matbaacılık ve Yayıncılık.

Turkish consciousness. But religion, which is a matter of conscience, is one thing, and *sharia*, which wants to keep society and world affairs within the conditions of the seventh century and freeze them, is another. The stigma of enmity against religion attached to Atatürk's revolutions is nothing but the slander of the enemies of civilization.

The founding period of the new Turkey has come to an end with these revolutions. But the revolutions we made were an act of "breaking the chains." The old-time and the old order, with their customs, traditions, and superstitious beliefs, were still present in the society. It was necessary to make the masses and the children of the people adopt the truths of the new time and the new order through a large-scale educational mobilization. Since the regime's destiny was to finally achieve the goal of "unconditional national sovereignty"—that is, democracy based on the will of the majority—we had to awaken this will and free it from the "old."

This has been the great flaw of the last period. Turkey was very late in its first educational work and could only reach the very edge of the Turkish villages. In his own words, Falih Rıfkı Atay remembers a discussion he had with Recep Peker in Rome. They had traveled there with İsmet Pasha, the Prime Minister. Recep Peker was the general clerk of the party. When he was talking about the brilliant achievements of the regime, Atay said, "Since the schools and teachers of this regime did not cover all the villages, we had done nothing." Peker was angry at Atay's exaggeration, and they argued for a while. For Atay, Peker was a very good-natured friend. His heart did not collect dust. After a while, Peker told Atay, "Falih, if you only knew how much I love you. Don't you have *Zeytindağı*? I always admired your views in that book." Atay replied, "My dear friend, when I collected the opinions in *Zeytindağı*, I was a young man of 22 or 23, and now I am 35 years old."[31] Atay states:

> It is our old disease to think that we have finished things with the law and to consider the issue as a matter of the upper floor of the society. Since the Tanzimat, an entire century has passed only by ventilating this upper floor. We did not think that, for eighty-five percent of the nation, not even a day had passed since the Tanzimat.

---

[31] Atay, F. R. (1999). *Çankaya*, Çağdaş Matbaacılık ve Yayıncılık.

By the second year of the revolution, Atay believed that many of those who had initially supported Atatürk and his vision were already growing restless. They sought ways to leave the country or secure comfortable, profitable positions within it. Atay states that the desire to escape to a European city, far from the devastated homeland and its impoverished people, to live a life of luxury with state cars and funds, or to exploit their influence in Çankaya for personal gain, was slowly eroding the revolutionary spirit. This pursuit of personal fortune began to infect the revolutionary heart of the movement. Atay often recalls the story from Cevdet's history of Selim III's reign, where the elite clung to their interests rather than the cause.

Atay observes that Atatürk, as a revolutionary leader, was like a commander without an army. After 1923, he had to fill the ranks of the provinces with loyal supporters. Yet, Atay points out, they rarely saw anyone approach Atatürk with the intention of serving the nation, and the small group of true believers in the revolution could not effectively carry forward the vision of the future. Atay asserts that the mission of the generation that came to power in 1923 was to help the people embrace Atatürk's reforms. He acknowledges that this was a challenging, often thankless task. Atay notes that many who passed these laws did not fully support them, and even the courts set up to punish those who resisted the reforms were not entirely sincere. He reflects that the new order's survival seemed to hinge on Atatürk himself. Atay recalls a conversation in Çankaya where one of Atatürk's friends said, "Think of your health, live long. After you're gone, they'll even tear down your statues."

Atay contends that those who call Atatürk's party a one-party system is mistaken. He states that the People's Party was a broad coalition, encompassing a range of ideologies—from the most conservative to the most progressive—while maintaining strict adherence to its core principles. Within this diverse party, Atay suggests, they often felt like outsiders. He recalls that they would sometimes advise Atatürk to expel those who didn't truly believe in the cause and surround himself with those who did. Atay believes that Atatürk placed his hopes in the youth of the Republic, believing they would help uplift the entire nation. During his travels to Russia, Atay struggled to explain to the authorities that there were faster and more efficient methods for educating the public and youth. He acknowledges that they could not fully grasp the advances and techniques of their time.

Atay concludes that, in the end, Atatürk did everything that could be expected of a reformist leader in the history of this nation. However, Atay believes that the intellectuals of the revolutionary period were less capable than any previous generation of effectively utilizing the influence and power that Atatürk had placed at their disposal for progressive causes. Atay adds that, despite Atatürk's brilliance, he also had shortcomings due to his upbringing. Unfortunately, Atay believes they could not address or overcome these deficiencies.[32]

Şükrü Hanioğlu, apart from his excellent book on *The late Ottoman Empire*,[33] has written two intellectual biographies of Mustafa Kemal Atatürk. These biographies have three main objectives. The first is to situate the founder of the modern Turkish Republic within his historical context. Atatürk did not wish to be seen as a solitary genius, unaffected by his upbringing, early social education, institutional affiliations, social environment, and intellectual influences. Additionally, his leadership in creating the Republic must be properly acknowledged. The second goal of this book is to trace Atatürk's intellectual development, which is the least explored aspect of his life and work. I can easily argue that he was an intellectual because his military and political thoughts had intellectual and, to some extent, philosophical depth. It is also important to examine Atatürk's views on religion in general and Islam in particular. The role of religion and secularism in politics and society was one of his major areas of interest. Still, the evolution of his ideas significantly impacted his political decisions and their implementations. The third is to analyze Atatürk's life, ideas, and work, including his historical experiences in the late Ottoman Empire and the Republic of Turkish State and the impact of his legacy on modern Turkey. These aspects should be seriously studied and published without making them legendary. On the contrary, they should be treated scientifically as the most significant historical ideas and decisions.

3.3.2. From Westernization to Turkish exceptionalism

We all know that the Ottomans and Turkey were under the restraint of paradoxical problems. Their sociopolitical and economic evolution had followed a

---

[32] Atay, F. R. (1999). *Çankaya*, Çağdaş Matbaacılık ve Yayıncılık.
[33] Şükrü Hanioğlu, M. (2008). *A Brief History of the Late Ottoman Empire*, pp. 6–212. Princeton: Princeton University Press.

different path from Europe's. The Ottomans have been undergoing a process of Westernization since the eighteenth century. Yet, profound differences in religious ideology, culture, sociopolitical systems, and statecraft have continued to separate the European and Ottoman worlds. Long before the Treaty of Westphalia (1648), when the European system was in its embryonic stage, the Ottoman Empire was an important factor in the European balance of power. Through its wars, alliances, and economic policies, it became deeply engaged in the continent's international affairs. The Ottoman Empire was formally included in the European system by the Treaty of Paris in 1856. However, the Ottoman state was already a dominant power until the Treaty of Karlowitz (1699), which marked a significant turning point in the military balance between Europe and the Ottoman Empire. After that date, the Ottoman state adopted a balance of power diplomacy, not to expand its influence and control in the West but to slow the pace of its decline. This policy was backed by European diplomacy, which sought to prevent the emergence of a dangerous power vacuum in the East that could result from the sudden collapse of the Empire. Consequently, reform became an element of policy not only by the Ottoman state but also, albeit hesitantly, for Europe. The Ottomans' recognition of European military superiority prepared the necessary psychological ground for the later cultural, administrative, and political borrowings from the West. The spread of the modernization process to areas beyond military institutions was equally inevitable.[34] Political modernization led to the adoption of the constitutional monarchy, briefly proclaimed in 1876 and reintroduced in 1908; it culminated in the establishment of the Turkish Republic in 1923 and the secularizing reforms of Atatürk. Ottoman leaders adopted secular laws and institutions without delay because, in any case, they had been used to the application of secular *kanunnames* of the sultans since the fifteenth century.

---

[34] Karaosmanoğlu, A. L. (1994). "The Limits of International Influence for Democratization," In M. Heper, and A. Evin (eds.), *Politics in the Third Turkish Republic*, pp. 117–131. Boulder and San Francisco: Westview Press; and Karaosmanoğlu, A. L. (1993). "Officers: Westernization and Democracy," In M. Heper, A. Öncü, and H. Kramer (eds.), *Turkey and the West: Changing Political and Cultural Identities*, pp. 19–34. London and New York: I.B. Tauris.

In order to reverse the process of disintegration, Ottoman reformers adopted two categories of modernizing measures. One category consisted of strengthening the armed forces and recentralizing the government. The government assumed a series of new responsibilities in fields such as education, law, trade, taxation, and agriculture; previously, most of these functions had been performed by local, communal, or religious institutions. Centralizing reforms were regarded as an essential means for effectively controlling the periphery. However, the resulting authoritarian system of government led not only to the differentiation and centralization of administrative functions essential for political modernization but also to a kind of "enlightened despotism," which later became the main target of the rising intelligentsia in Europe and the Ottoman Empire. The second group of measures concerned improving the status of both the Muslim and non-Muslim subjects of the Empire to satisfy demands for equality, land ownership, and improving individuals' status before the state. At the outset, these two types of measures were considered necessary to ward off foreign encroachments. Over time, they gradually evolved into two complementary, but at times contradictory, approaches to modernization, which continued to mark the process of democratization in Turkey.[35]

After the failure of the Ottoman military force in the Balkan Wars, it improved itself significantly within one year and reached the level of winning quite a number of battles against the European powers during World War I. However, it lost the First World War together with Germany. Following that defeat, the Turks fought against the Western occupation. The War of Independence (1919–1922), however, did not aim to distance Turkey from Western principles of government or European economic and social systems. On the contrary, creating a modern nation-state with a Western type of polity was a struggle. The Republican reforms to establish such a polity were initiated under a mildly authoritarian single-party regime, whose leaders preferred to exercise "controlled political intimidation" rather than resort to repression. The Kemalist revolution, which took on the characteristics of an elite movement, sought to suppress symbols of the Ottoman *ancien régime.* At the same time, however, the Kemalist movement paved the way—even if

---

[35]   Mardin, S. (1971). "Ideology and Religion in the Turkish Revolution," *International Journal of Middle East Studies*, 2, 198–199.

indirectly—for later structural changes such as the gradual rise of a bourgeoisie, the emergence of a labor movement, the growth of municipal autonomy, the liberalization of the economy, and related political and economic processes. At this point, we must reconsider Şerif Mardin's concept of "Turkish exceptionalism" by referring to some of his excellent explanations:

> The modernization of Turkey is usually covered as a process primarily generated after the foundation of the Turkish Republic. This is a clearly simplistic image that neglects to bring in the continuities between the nineteenth-century Tanzimat reforms and the Republic itself. These continuities may even be traced to the earlier rise of a Turkish bureaucratic class (circa 1780). Another aspect of this simplification is that it neglects the type of institution-building policy that goes back to the reign of Sultan Abdulhamid II (1876-1909) and the type of synthesis between Islam and modernity that was promoted by an intellectual elite between 1908 and 1923... The ubiquity of a peculiar mix of state and religious discourse in the Ottoman Empire promoted a modern Turkish Islamic "exceptionalism" with distant Ottoman roots. It is the concentration of Islamic studies on the Islam of Arabs that has hidden this character of Ottoman religious structure—a character that antedates and adumbrates the secularism of the Turkish Republic.[36]

Turkish Exceptionalism is the result of a *praxis*, an ethical political decision, and its application in order to avoid political clashes and other inconveniences. Although we may underline that this praxis is the guarantee of a rightful operation, Mardin suggests that the continuity of this praxis was disrupted by the Nakşibendi Sufi orders, which, like all Islamic brotherhoods, used networks organizing for their own praxis. Codes are used as symbols to represent social reality and institution-building. Mardin also refers to another specific type of praxis for dealing with social reality in the Soviet Union of Russia: *the Operational Code of the Politburo,* which appears in the title of a book by Nathan Leites.[37] Mardin's book aims not to explore the major theories of Leninism-Stalinism but to uncover the principles that the Bolsheviks considered essential for effective political conduct. His book focuses primarily on the relationship between the Party and the external world rather than

---

[36] Mardin, S. (1971). "Ideology and Religion in the Turkish Revolution," *International Journal of Middle East Studies*, 2, 198–199.

[37] Leites, N. (1951). *The Operational Code of the Politburo.* Santa Monica: The RAND Corporation; new ed. 2007.

the Party's internal dynamics. Mardin notes that this represents a specific type of praxis of dealing with social reality. It somewhat resembles the praxis of Ottoman bureaucrats and those of the Turkish Republic. Some excellent historians are very much interested in the similarities between Russia and Turkey. The Late Norman Stone is one of them.

Regarding "reconstruction," each of these codes changed over time, eventually converging toward the area of politics. "Exceptionalism" is how a very special dialectic has marked Islam in the Ottoman Empire and Turkey. Their characteristics worked cumulatively to create a unique setting for Islam, where secularism and Islam interpenetrate. This was not a fusion of secularism and religion but a concentration of social movements as cognitive practice. The history of modern Turkey is not a conflict between republicanism and Sultanism, nor a struggle defined by Islam and secularism. Charles Taylor's focus on the implicit agreement of shared beliefs is crucial in this context.[38] Over a long history, the imbrications of Islam with civil society suggest something beyond structural characteristics. They have been useful explanatory variables, which are more profound than eventful occasions. Religion and the self are brought together in the same scope. This means that the dialectic has worked but without fusion.[39]

Mustafa Kemal Atatürk differed from many of his peers and friends on two fundamental issues: one was the role of the military in society; the other was the role and position of religions in internal and international relations. Though he approved of von der Goltz Pasha's strategic ideas in general, he did not consider the paramilitary organizational model of the Committee of Union and Progress (CUP) suitable for creating an Ottoman-Turkish nation in arms. Atatürk never forgot the successful and unsuccessful experiences

---

[38] Taylor, C. (1984). *Philosophy and the Human Sciences.* Cambridge: Cambridge University Press, 1985.

[39] Mardin, S. (June 2005). "Turkish Islamic Exceptionalism Yesterday and Today: Continuity, Rupture and Reconstruction in Operational Codes," *Turkish Studies* (Routledge), 6(2), 145–165; Leites, N. (1951). *The Operational Code of the Politburo.* Santa Monica: The RAND Corporation; new ed. 2007; Stone, N. (2004). "Turkey in the Russian Mirror." In J. Erickson (ed.), *Russia: War, Peace and Diplomacy*, pp. 86–102. Great Britain: Weidenfeld and Nicolson.

of the CUP leader Enver Pasha.[40] Although Mustafa Kemal was an advocate for Westernization, he was also a strong opponent of the increasing foreign influence, particularly Germany, on the army. He praised Goltz's contribution to the development of the Ottoman military but was seriously critical of the German military reform mission and its leader, Liman von Sanders. In the second half of the nineteenth century, some radical Young Turk groups favored the German doctrines known as *Vulgarmaterialismus.*

This was a distorted version of materialism, blending popular ideas of materialism, scientism, and Darwinism into a simplistic belief system that reinforced the role of a self-proclaimed science in society. Though they were a marginal group at the turn of the century, the Young Turks were destined to govern the Islamic caliphate for nearly a decade and later shape a secular nation-state from its remnants. Thus, Şükrü Hanioğlu confirms that the German doctrine of *Vulgarmaterialismus* became the ideological pillar of the modern republican Turkish nation-state. Following this confirmation, Hanioğlu added:

> It is impossible to understand the politics of Mustafa Kemal without recognizing that he belonged to the educated class of a generation that embraced a crude conception of science as a panacea for the ills of the Empire and saw in the doctrine of vulgar materialism an indispensable manual for constructing a prosperous, rational, and irreligious modern society.[41]

We do not have to study again the transition from the Ottoman Empire to the Republic of Turkey in terms of security and secularism. We have already examined these aspects in detail and depth; we know that Mustafa Kemal Atatürk has been familiarized with the political and philosophical knowledge of von der Goltz Pasha and Clausewitz. Goltz Pash's opus work, *Millet-i Müselleha* (Ordu Millet), was full of references to Clausewitz. Thus, the most significant and fundamental result of Goltz Pash's lessons was the military

---

[40] Şükrü Hanioğlu, M. (2011). *Atatürk: An Intellectual Biography*, pp. 45–47. Princeton: Princeton University Press.

[41] Şükrü Hanioğlu, M. (2011). *Atatürk: An Intellectual Biography*, pp. 49–50. Princeton: Princeton University Press. See also Hanioğlu's more detailed chapter on the same topic in *Atatürk: Entelektüel Biyografi* (Chapter 3) (2023), "Jön Türklerin Bilimciliği ve Bilimcilerin Garpçılığı", pp. 119–174. İstanbul: Bağlam Yayıncılık.

strategic knowledge in both war and peace imparted to Mustafa Kemal and his contemporaries. Now, it is time to address the perspectives of two other prominent Republican political scientists on secularism and laicism: Şerif Mardin and Andrew Davison.

In our study of Mardin's ideas, we will remain within the framework of his book, which is notably above average in quality, relating to *Religion, Society, and Modernity in Turkey*.[42] It would be incorrect to confine modern Turkish history exclusively within the context of the state's secular policies. Secular policies can be traced back to the fifteenth century in the Ottoman Empire. The development of Islamic thought from 1908 to 1922 can also be connected to Abdülhamid II's earlier Ottomanization–Islamization policies. In early republican Turkey, the population still largely came from peasant backgrounds, and the provisional centers that had emerged during the Hamidian era supported Mustafa Kemal. The prevailing belief among the local leadership at the time appeared to be that the brave generals and allies of Mustafa Kemal aimed to preserve the Sultanate and enhance the prestige of Islam. This belief was not entirely incorrect, as Mustafa Kemal did not initially show much interest in Islamic matters, such as the translation of original people's dialectical languages and the regional vernaculars of the Qur'an. It may have been that he heard the vernacular of Islam as a means of mobilizing a rural population; this aim became far less appealing following the Kurdish rebellion of 1925.

According to Şerif Mardin, there is no doubt that Mustafa Kemal sought to utilize Islam as a means of fostering civil participation. The key elements of this project included bridging the divide between the religion of the elite and that of the general populace. This approach continued the Young Turks' focus on spreading religious truths (*hakaik-i diniye*) and the high ideals of Islam (*me'ali-yi Islamiye*) to the broader population (*neşr ve tamim*), a task the Young Turks had entrusted to the Foundation for Islamic Knowledge (*Dar-ül Hikmet-i Islamiye*) in 1918. Islam as a vehicle for civility reappears when examining the profiles of those appointed by Mustafa Kemal to the Directorate General of Religious Affairs between 1924 and 1938. Mustafa Kemal's practical goals are reflected in his policies of "Turkification" of

---

[42] Mardin, S. (2006). *Religion, Society, and Modernity in Turkey*, pp. 225–315. Syracuse, NY: Syracuse University Press.

Islamic rituals. The secularization policies of the Republic, already evident in the Republican People's Party statutes of September 9, 1923, should be analyzed alongside Mustafa Kemal's efforts to adapt Islam for republican purposes. The gradual decline of this utilitarian policy in the late 1920s and 1930s still requires study from this dual perspective to understand the origins and development of secularization during this period.[43]

Ziya Gökalp was another leading Ottoman and Republican intellectual with a profound understanding of the Western World and Islam. He carried out a "sociological-Durkheimian" analysis of religion. However, Gökalp's belief that Turkey's progress would involve modernization alongside "Turkification" and "Islamization" has had a profound impact on Turkey, fostering a nationalist-Islamic synthesis. This concept later laid the foundation for a revised platform for the Nationalist Action Party in the 1980s. In the same decade, Hüseyin Kazım Kadri, a former Young Turk who later aligned with religious sympathizers, offered a systematic critique of Gökalp's religio-nationalist synthesis in 1989.

> Once again, one cannot speak of the revival of Islam in Turkey without noticing the overlap between Islam and nationalism. The Second Constitutional Period had been one during which a wide-ranging debate discussed the interrelation of Turkishness, modernism, and Islam. The competition to compose a Turkish national anthem, set by the Turkish Republic, was won by the Islamist intellectual Mehmet Akif and adopted by the Grand National Assembly in 1921. Today, it is still one of the most revered elements in the expression of national sentiment in Turkey.[44]

Now comes *Center-Periphery as a Concept for the Study of Social Transformation*: Generally, society has a center. Certain societies have stronger centers than others. The Ottoman Empire had emerged as an outstanding exception, thanks to a lasting center supported by a sophisticated network of institutions. As we have already studied, Fatih Sultan Mehmet and the following sultans developed and effectively controlled the balance of power between the two rival institutions: the Autonomous Provincial Administrations and the

---

[43] Mardin, S. (2006). *Religion, Society, and Modernity in Turkey*, p. 278. Syracuse, NY: Syracuse University Press.
[44] Mardin, S. (2006). *Religion, Society, and Modernity in Turkey*, pp. 278–279. NY: Syracuse University Press.

Janissary Corps. Before the nineteenth century, the characteristics of multiple confrontations and integrations appear to be absent in the Ottoman Empire. Instead, the primary conflict was unidimensional, consistently between the center and the periphery. Mardin argues that the center-periphery opposition became a central issue in Ottoman political and economic life for various reasons. One such reason was the tension between urban populations and the large, persistent groups of nomads in Anatolia, the Empire's heartland.[45]

Translating the Qur'an into Turkish was seen as a necessary step for literate Turkish Muslims to comprehend. This effort began in the nineteenth century and continued into the twentieth century, with notable contributions from the Tatar scholar Musa Carullah Bigi (1875–1949). Ziya Gökalp shared a similar view, but he believed that Turkish, the language or dialect spoken by the common people, would be insufficient for religious discourse unless it could connect with the broader Muslim cultural context. In the early years of the Republic, some Turkish intellectuals, encouraged by Mustafa Kemal, aimed to create a Turkish translation of the Qur'an. Among them were İsmail Hakkı İzmirli and Mehmet Akif. However, in a February 5, 1933 speech, Mustafa Kemal emphasized the cultural importance of the issue within the Republic. He stated that this is not a matter of religion; it is a matter of language. It must be understood clearly that the foundation of the Turkish nation lies in its national language and identity. This particular point was the only one that gained broad public support.[46]

3.4. Reorganization of the Army

3.4.1. Atatürk's intellectual trajectory from the empire to the republic

Turkish democracy began to take shape in the late 1940s with the approval of the Armed Forces. Since then, the political process has experienced three military interventions: in 1960, 1971–1973, and 1980–1983. Despite these interventions, the Turkish officer corps has shown the characteristics of an

---

[45]   Mardin, S. (2006). *Religion, Society, and Modernity in Turkey*. NY: Syracuse University Press.

[46]   Mardin, S. (2006). *Religion, Society, and Modernity in Turkey*, pp. 298–327. NY: Syracuse University Press.

"arbitrator army."[47] They have always reiterated their reluctance to become directly involved in politics, yet they view themselves as the guardians of the state and Kemalist principles. Since the officers have emerged as the primary Westernizers in Turkish history, it is important to understand their perception of the West. We may safely assume that, for the contemporary Turkish officer (mostly the army's general staff), Westernization implies democratization. Even if this assumption is correct, it is insufficient to explain the problematic role played by the officers in the democratization process. Another important aspect of this study is to show how encounters with the West have shaped Western conceptions of the military profession and politico-strategic culture. To accomplish this, we must conduct a historical and philosophical analysis of early encounters, which seem to have left a segmented conception of the West. We should then attempt to explain the Turkish officers' frame of mind to be better prepared for discussing certain recent trends that may contribute to resolving these paradoxes within the Republic of Turkey.

The Treaty of Karlowitz (1699) marked the beginning of the Ottoman Empire's moderate decline in its relations with Europe. The military defeats led the imperial elite to seek the cause of the decline in the military superiority of their European adversaries and to accept the desirability of borrowing new forms of military organization, techniques, and weapons from Europe. They established close contacts with European capitals, such as Paris, Vienna, and London, by sending envoys and accepting European ambassadors to İstanbul. The function of these Ottoman envoys was not only to negotiate and conclude treaties but also to send information back to the capital about European political and military affairs: "This was the first breach in the Ottoman iron curtain, a concession to the reality that the Ottomans could no longer afford to ignore internal developments in Europe."[48] Without correcting this argument, I do not want to continue. At the same time, the following explanations will further clarify the Ottoman and European relationship.

Mesut Uyar and Edward J. Erickson, in their Military History Book, have included strategic effectiveness in the Chapter entitled "*The Nizam-ı Cedid*

---

[47] Perlmutter, A. (1978). *The Military and Politics in Modern Times*, p. 104. New Haven, CT: Yale University Press.

[48] Shaw, S. J. (1976). *History of the Ottoman Empire and Modern Turkey: The Rise and Decline of the Ottoman Empire, 1280–1808*, p.233. Cambridge: Cambridge University Press.

Reforms.[49] Sultan Selim III was still partially satisfied by the strategic ideas of his advisers. He continued to seek first-hand information about military advancements in Europe. As a result of his understanding, Sultan Selim III decided to send Ebubekir Ratip Efendi to Vienna as an ambassador to collect military information for the Sultan and the Ottoman Armed Forces. Ratip Efendi delivered the most important strategic and reform reports in November 1971 and September 1792. Sultan Selim struggled to unite the factions within the reformist camp as rival groups undermined each other's efforts. Amid this turmoil, Ratip Efendi was also removed from the scene. It was under these chaotic conditions that a minor disturbance among the guards of the Istanbul Straits quickly escalated into a full-scale rebellion on May 25, 1807. During the *Vaka-i Hayriyye*, which aimed to eliminate the Janissaries, their destruction removed the final major obstacle to modernization and initiated a period of reform. As a result, the Ottoman military adopted a European-style regular army supported by a reserve system.

The *Sefaretname* (ambassadorial report) of Ratip Efendi and the military reforms of Selim III were not the only encounters with the West. Several European converts who worked for the Ottomans as administrators and soldiers in the eighteenth century provided a different perspective on the West. Officers like Comte de Bonneval (1675–1747) and Baron François de Tott (1730–1793) played key roles in introducing European military techniques to the Ottomans, establishing modern military schools, and reorganizing the army. As men of the Enlightenment, they believed that reason should guide all aspects of life, including military affairs. "They showed a yearning for the idea of rational inquiry with the maximum mathematical precision and certainty possible."[50] As a result, in the eighteenth century, the Ottoman military witnessed the emergence of the military schools (*Hendesehane and Mühendishane*), the rapid-fire artillery corps, new training techniques, and serious efforts to restructure the entire military establishment, including

---

[49] Uyar, M., and Erickson, E. J. (2019). *A Military History of the Ottomans from Osman to Atatürk*, pp. 1–128.

[50] Gat, A. (1989). *The Origins of Military Thought from the Enlightenment to Clausewitz*, pp. 13–28. Oxford: Clarendon Press.

the navy, along French and Austrian lines.[51] In addition to these reforms, the notion emerged that the army profession could be studied in theory and thus necessitated academic training. [52]

In the eighteenth century, however, Europeans began to witness the rise of a genuine philosophical movement and its impact on the military field. In Europe, a reaction formed against the ideas of the radical Enlightenment. The intellectual premises that had guided the military thinkers of that period were seen as seriously superficial and pretentious. Clausewitz (1780–1831) expressed the most reinforced disapproval, emphasizing the significance of national characteristics, political situations, customs, culture, and history. Thus, rejecting the Enlightenment's universal abstractions in favor of a belief in historical diversity and the complexity of social and political forms became one of the dominant themes of the real German philosophical movement.[53] The Ottoman military reformers, however, took their cues from the innovations introduced by the French Enlightenment. Neither the German philosophical movement nor the British conservatism of Edmund Burke had an impact on their intellectual formation. Early encounters with the West led the Ottoman military to misconceive the real nature of European thought as manifested in British conservatism and the German philosophical movement, which had developed as derivatives of the philosophical debate between the intellectual traditions of the Enlightenment and those of the Counter-Enlightenment. This real philosophical debate, however, did not stop the adoption of positivist ideas toward the end of the nineteenth century. Positivism was viewed as a crucial idea for countering religious fanaticism. This is reflected in Atatürk's words: "… bear in mind that Turkey cannot be a country of apostles, saints, clergy, and fanatics. The truest guide in life is science."[54]

---

[51] Shaw, S. J. (1976). *History of the Ottoman Empire and Modern Turkey: The Rise and Decline of the Ottoman Empire, 1280–1808*, pp. 240–277. Cambridge: Cambridge University Press.

[52] Gat, A. (1989). *The Origins of Military Thought from the Enlightenment to Clausewitz*, p. 59. Oxford: Clarendon Press.

[53] Gat, A. (1989). *The Origins of Military Thought from the Enlightenment to Clausewitz*, p. 187. Oxford: Clarendon Press.

[54] Atatürk'ün Söylev ve Demeçler, vol. II (1959), p. 215, cited in Mardin S. (1981). "Atatürk and Positivist Thought," In *Atatürk and Turkey of the Republican Era*, p. 60. Ankara: Turkish Union of Chambers.

The positivist approach to social affairs was emphasized as a tool for reorganizing society to ensure the state's preservation. In this approach, the state is conceived as an abstract entity, divorced from society as well as from the individual. The modern conception of the state was neglected in the modern German philosophical arguments; it was inherent in the centralized aspect of the Ottoman Empire. However, we know that the Ottoman social-political organization, the Empire, had quite a number of autonomous administrative entities within its territories.

Positivism continued to be an important idea propagated by the Young Turks and was an important aspect of a Turkish officer's thought pattern. In Atatürk's opinion, the limits of individual freedom were to be determined according to scientific principles. Moreover, protecting individual freedoms should be important to defend the will and sovereignty of the state. Today, for many officers, democracy is a tool for safeguarding and advancing the state. It should offer a structure for constructive discussion aimed at finding rational solutions to societal, political, and economic challenges. The Turkish officer seems to have considerable difficulty perceiving democracy as a regime in which public policies are made through the reconciliation of conflicting interests. The existence of various interest groups and their "irresponsible wrangling with each other" was regarded by officers as one of the major issues in Turkish democracy, and it was seen as a contributing factor to the military interventions.[55]

A Turkish officer's early encounter with the misleading outward appearance of the Enlightenment, combined with the social architecture side of Ottoman statecraft, has given him a purely rationalistic and positivistic approach to social and political affairs. He was the first to be Westernized and was the master Westernizer of polity and society. His other mission has been to defend the country against internal and external enemies, and those who rejected Westernization are viewed as among the major internal enemies. On the other hand, the West itself was, for a long time, the mightiest external enemy of all.

---

[55] Batur, M., & ve Görüşler V. (1985) [*Memoirs and Opinions*], İstanbul: Milliyet Yayınları, p. 192. General (ret.) Batur was the former Commander-in-Chief of the Air Force and one of the leaders of the 1971–1973 military intervention in politics.

In the process, Turkish officers promoted three conflicting and paradoxical political ideas: The military maintained a stance of staying out of governmental politics to preserve its professional integrity, intervening only when necessary to protect the secular and democratic regime. While contributing to democratization as a key aspect of Westernization, it refrained from becoming an instrument of government policy. At the same time, it sought to join the Western community of nations, aiming to become an integral part of it while also continuing military and political precautions against the West. Nevertheless, certain developments in the early years of Republican Turkey began to relent these paradoxes. We can say that the fundamental formal disappearance of these paradoxes took place after the 1980s. Chief of General Staff Necip Torumtay's response to press speculation that his resignation had been prompted by a military-civilian conflict is an indication of this transformation: "There is no conflict between the military and civilian officials. The Turkish Armed Forces commanders know very well that the civilian authority always has the final word. The Army knows where it stands…"[56]

3.4.2. Atatürk and Goltz Pasha

There is no doubt that Andrew Mango[57] is one of the leading writers who completed the biography of the founder of the Republic of Turkey. He clearly and in detail points out that Mustafa Kemal never supported the CUP and the Young Turk movement with sympathy.

"The Young Turk Revolution was a messy affair."[58] It was a spontaneous combat rather than a carefully planned military operation. Mustafa Kemal and his friends were educated in modern military schools; they were young and trained military officers. On June 22, 1908, just before the Young Turk Revolution, Mustafa Kemal was appointed an inspector for the railway line running from Salonica to Ürgüp (Skopje). Mustafa Kemal's dear friend Ali Fuat was appointed to a similar job between Salonica and Manastır. Ali Fuat later said, "Appointment as a guide meant in those days that one was out of

---

[56] *Dateline* (15 December 1990), p. 2.

[57] Mango, A. (2000). *Atatürk: The Biography of the Founder of Modern Turkey*, pp. 19, 49, 90, 101, 131, 154, 159. New York: The Overlook Press.

[58] Mango, A. (2000). *Atatürk: The Biography of the Founder of Modern Turkey*, pp. 74–76. New York: The Overlook Press.

favor with the leadership. In our case, the reason was that we both believed that the revolutionary policy of the society was inadequate. We used to say this and express criticism in secret meetings." However, Mustafa Kemal voiced his criticism not only in covert gatherings but also during lively debates over drinks in cafés.

In March 1914, Mustafa Kemal attained the rank of Lieutenant Colonel. This promotion did not change his duties in Bulgaria, where he was a military attaché, primarily dealing with intelligence. Mustafa Kemal's resources were limited, so he requested the necessary funds from his superiors in Bulgaria to improve his access to intelligence resources. After his success, he reported that the chief of the Bulgarian general staff had informed him that German officers, especially Goltz Pasha, had shared information with the Bulgarians regarding the movements of Ottoman military units. Kazım Karabekir, appointed to the 2nd Intelligence Department of the Ottoman general staff in January 1914, warned Mustafa Kemal that his reports had provoked the German general overseeing the department. In response, Mustafa Kemal expressed surprise at this information, noting that a recent letter from Istanbul had clarified the matter and resolved any misunderstanding. He stressed that his only objective was to serve his country, making the German officer's reaction unjustified.[59]

Mustafa Kemal was wary of the Bulgarians. In a detailed analysis written in Sofia and his lectures, he emphasized that they still aspired to reclaim Edirne. He argued that the Ottomans should counter this by improving officer training and fostering a spirit of initiative and offensive strategy. This perspective aligned closely with the views of the German military mission, particularly those of von der Goltz. Enver Pasha approved it without hesitation. Thus, the political gap between Mustafa Kemal and von der Goltz was closing rapidly but unobtrusively. Conversely, in Gallipoli, relations between Mustafa Kemal and Liman von Sanders worsened without hope for future improvement. When World War I began, Mustafa Kemal expected an appointment in Macedonia. However, he was offered command in Mesopotamia, where British troops under General Townshend had invaded Kut al-Amarah and prepared to threaten Baghdad. Mustafa Kemal agreed on the condition that

---

[59] Mango, A. (2000). *Atatürk: The Biography of the Founder of Modern Turkey*, p. 131, New York: The Overlook Press.

he be appointed both military commander and governor-general of all Iraq, with the authority to select his own staff. However, this arrangement was never realized. Mustafa Kemal's hopes were disappointed. The command in Mesopotamia was assigned to the aging German Marshal von der Goltz Pasha. Mustafa Kemal appeared to have anticipated this decision or a comparable high-ranking appointment. He sent a letter to his friend Salih (Bozok) in Istanbul, reiterating that the British enemy in Iraq was exhausted and would soon be expelled from the area. This was also the view of von der Goltz.

However, the 16th Corps remained under the command of Liman von Sanders, who was eager to launch an offensive against the Allies in Macedonia as soon as possible. His proposal lacked support from the German high command, while the Ottoman high command had other strategic priorities. Under von der Goltz's command, German-led operations were well shielded from danger and risk. Townshend's advance was halted at the Battle of Salman Pak on November 25, 1915, and his retreating forces were encircled at Kut al-Amarah by Ottoman troops led by von der Goltz Pasha. Goltz passed away from typhus on April 19, 1916. Ten days later, Townshend surrendered at Kut to the new Turkish commander, Enver's uncle Halil Pasha.[60] The Ottoman Imperial Army housed the British general in a richly decorated residence on the Princes' Islands until the end of World War I.

The French defeat by Prussia in 1870–1871 sparked a greater interest in German military instruction. In 1883–1884, at the sultan's request, the renowned German General Colmar von der Goltz oversaw restructuring the Ottoman Royal Military Academy and other military schools, basing them on German institutions. Goltz emphasized the teaching of algebra, mathematics, and related technical subjects, gradually establishing a new ethic of service and military discipline, which the Young Turk movements had weakened. He also advocated for a more prominent role for the military in society. Mustafa Kemal and his friends, who waged the War of Independence with great success, had been educated in the Ottoman military schools and Royal Military Academies that Goltz Pasha had helped to establish. It was both ironic and understandable that Goltz's ideas had a greater influence on the Ottoman Empire than in his native Germany. His worldview shaped the

---

[60] Mango, A. (2000). *Atatürk: The Biography of the Founder of Modern Turkey*, pp. 54–159. New York: The Overlook Press.

perspectives of many Ottoman officers who studied the Turkish edition of *Das Volk in Waffen* at the Royal Military Academy starting in 1886. Mustafa Kemal believed that the advancement of the Turkish military would cultivate a stronger sense of Turkish national identity within society. His Turkish sympathies also prompted him to decrease the importance of military Westernization. Mustafa Kemal was a fervent opponent of the growing influence of foreigners, especially Germany, on the Ottoman army. There is no doubt that he always praised Goltz's contributions to the development of the Ottoman military.

Like many colleagues, Mustafa Kemal shared Colmar von der Goltz's view that "to make war means to attack." In one of his essays, he said, "The army must be the army of offense. Our weapons are good not for defending ourselves from the enemy but for making the enemy shield himself against us." Many strategists of the period shared similar views. However, implementing these principles was nearly impossible for the Ottomans at the time, with a few exceptions. One exception was the Crimean War of 1853–1856, during which the Ottomans were an important ally to European states. Another exception was the Ottoman-Greek War of 1897, a relatively small-scale conflict against a weak third-tier power. Mustafa Kemal argued that only nations motivated by the Japanese attack code of "kögeki seishin" (aggressive spirit) could effectively carry out offensive wars. In 1914, however, the Ottoman military lacked a fully developed fighting spirit. Despite this, during the first two years of the Great War, the Ottoman armies managed to summon the determination to fight, even if it meant embracing extreme and radical interpretations of von der Goltz Pasha's ideas. Until then, we will regard the new military as an isolated elite, distinct from the general population—arrogant, Westernized, and driven by ambition. Mustafa Kemal and his colleagues' education at the Royal Military Academy positioned them as respected members of this emerging class, capable of guiding Goltz's "nation in arms" doctrine. While they shared many of Goltz Pasha's strategic views, the new Ottoman officer class had one significant reservation: they felt that Pasha's doctrine was being presented as the original model of an ideal nation-state, Germany. By contrast, the Ottoman state was an empire coming apart along its autonomous or semi-autonomous entities (provincial and provisional administrations). A nationalist ideology would likely be more successful in an ethnically homogeneous population, and Mustafa Kemal proposed bold ideas along these lines. As early as 1907, he suggested that the Ottoman Empire should voluntarily dissolve, enabling population exchanges that would pave the way for the creation of a Turkish state. His vision was of a "Turkish Nation in arms." However, with the outbreak of the First World War in 1914, it was too premature and strategically imprudent to try to reshape the Ottoman army into this ideal. This had implications not only for military effectiveness but also for political decision-making, as Goltz's followers, including Mustafa Kemal, believed they had the right to influence key political matters through the power of the military institution. During the First World War, Mustafa Kemal was in command of various institutions, military operations, and battles in the service of the Ottoman Army. He showed exceptional military and political qualities as a great commander in critical geographic, political, and risky areas such as the Balkans, Iraq, and the Dardanelles.[61]

Lt. Col. Edward J. Erickson, US Army (retired), wrote quite a number of articles and books on Ottoman and Turkish military history. One of his recent works is *Ottoman Army Effectiveness in World War I*.[62] In that book, Erickson wrote many paragraphs about Field Marshal Colmar von der Goltz. Generally, most of these paragraphs were on the army reorganization. The reorganization of the Ottoman Army brought significant changes to its command structure. Equally important was the comprehensive restructuring of the infantry division, which was based on Colmar von der Goltz's tactical principles. This realignment brought the Ottoman Army in line with the operational and tactical doctrines of contemporary European forces. These changes were put into effect in September 1910, following the annual fall maneuvers. The most notable transformation occurred at the division level, an idea believed to have been initiated by von der Goltz, who advocated for offensives supported by direct artillery at the tactical level. On July 10, 1910, the army issued its reorganization instructions (*Devlet-i Aliyye-i Osmaniye Ordusunun Teşkilât-ı Esasiye Nizamnamesi*), marking the adoption of the European army corps system with slight adjustments. The most radical reform was at the division level, where, influenced by von der Goltz's tactical ideas,

---

[61] For this paradoxical situation, see Şükrü Hanioğlu, M. (2011). *Atatürk: An Intellectual Biography*, pp. 33–38, 41–43, 71–78. Princeton: Princeton University Press.

[62] Erickson, E. J. (2007). *Ottoman Army Effectiveness in World War I*. New York and Canada: Routledge.

the Ottoman General Staff decided to remove two infantry brigade head-quarters from its divisions.

After the Absolute defeat of Napoleon in 1815, the empires of Europe confronted the emergence of nationalism on a wide scale, including the Ottoman Empire. All of Sultan Mahmud II's high officials and high-ranking Janissary officials had approved the project on May 28, 1826. The project initially proposed a limited reform and sought merely a legitimate reason to eliminate the Janissaries once and for all. The Janissary leaders immediately opposed any attempts at reform. In response, Sultan Mahmud II acted swiftly and decisively against the rebels on June 15, 1826. Key officials and loyal Janissary officers rallied around the sultan. At the same time, many members of the Kapıkulu and Ulema mobilized the civilian population, turning them against the Janissaries, who were caught off guard and unprepared. After the first clashes, the primary group of rebels was completely wiped out. Although the reformers focused on technological improvements, they failed to fully consider the political, social, and economic implications of such a major structural change, which at the time seemed primarily a military matter. Over time, this neglect (or ignorance) was replaced by increasing social and political interest in economics and geography. Nevertheless, von der Goltz and Mustafa Kemal have always been in favor of the replacement, virtually, that is, in effect, though not in name.[63]

The Ottomans and the Turkish Republic did not find a direct opportunity to read Clausewitz in detail. After the Treaty of Karlowitz (1699), the Ottoman Empire began to decline slowly in its relations with Europe. Military defeats and territorial losses led the imperial elite to seek the causes of the decline in the military superiority of their European adversaries and to recognize the need to adopt new forms of military organization, techniques, and weapons from Europe. They began to establish contact with European ambassadors in İstanbul and to send Ottoman envoys to European capitals, such as Paris and Vienna. The function of these envoys was not only to negotiate and conclude treaties but also to send information back to their own capital about European

---

[63] Erickson, E. J. (2007). *Ottoman Army Effectiveness in World War I*, pp. 55–57, 66–96, 178–180. New York and Canada: Routledge. See also Uyar, M. and Erickson, E. J. (2009). *A Military History of the Ottomans: From Osman to Atatürk*, pp. 120–130. Oxford: Oxford University Press.

political and military affairs. I do not want to conclude this paragraph without repeating a critical argument of mine: there was never an "Ottoman and European iron curtain" in history. They always existed between them mutual friendship and mutual antagonism. However, they always needed each other and tried to get over this paradox. For instance, Sultan Selim III's (1789–1807) envoy to Vienna, Ebubekir Ratip Efendi, included in his reports detailed accounts of the organizational structure of the Austrian military and the techniques used by Western forces. He referred to Raimondo Montecuccoli (1609–1680) as the most distinguished modern military thinker. Ratip Efendi's reference to Montecuccoli was significant. The Italian general who served Austria was an early representative of Enlightenment military thought. He advocated a systematic approach to military organization and the conduct of war, presenting decimal arithmetic, the calculation of spaces, and the use of geometrical methods and trigonometry as essential knowledge for the art of war. The reports of Ratip Efendi and the military reforms of Selim III were not the Ottomans' only encounters with the West,[64] but at the same time, it was too late for a considerable military reform.

Towards the end of the eighteenth century, however, Europeans began to witness the rise of the German philosophical movement and its impact on the military field. In Europe, a reaction began to form against the ideas of the radical Enlightenment; the intellectual premises that had guided the military thinkers of that period were seriously questioned as superficial and pretentious. This reaction, reinforced by disillusionment with the French Revolution, found its most developed form of expression in the works of Clausewitz (1780–1831). In contrast to the universal standards employed by the men of the Enlightenment, Clausewitz emphasized national characteristics, the political situation, customs, culture, and history. Thus, rejecting the universal abstractions of the Enlightenment in favor of a belief in historical diversity and the complexity of societal and political forms became one of the dominant themes of the German philosophical movement.

The Ottoman military reformers, however, were also influenced by the innovations brought about by the French Enlightenment. Neither the German philosophical movement nor the British conservatism of Edmund

---

[64] Karal, E. Z. (1988). *Selim III'ün Hatt-ı Hümâyunları, 1789–1807*, pp. 31–34. Ankara: Türk Tarih Kurumu.

Burke impacted their intellectual formation. Early encounters with the West led the Ottoman military to misconceive the real nature of European thought, as manifested in British conservatism and the German philosophical movement, which had developed as derivatives of the philosophical debate between the intellectual tradition of the Enlightenment and the Counter-Enlightenment. Despite the arrival in Turkey of German military experts in the late nineteenth and early twentieth centuries and the general staff training devised by General Colmar von der Goltz, this misconception continued to dominate. It was accentuated by the adoption of positivist ideas towards the end of the nineteenth century. Positivism was seen as an essential tool to combat religious extremism. This again is reflected in Atatürk's words: "... bear in mind that Turkey cannot be a country of apostles, saints, clergy, and fanatics. The trusted guide in life is science."

A Turkish officer's early encounter with the misleading outward appearance of the Enlightenment, combined with the social architecture side of Ottoman statecraft, has given a purely rationalistic and positivistic approach to social and political affairs. He was the first to be Westernized and was the first Westernizer of polity and society. His other mission has been to defend the country against internal as well as external enemies, with those who rejected Westernization considered among the major internal enemies. On the other hand, the West was sometimes becoming the mightiest external enemy of all.[65] The longstanding antagonistic relations between the Ottoman Empire and Christian Europe were not only a conflict of interest but also a clash of hostile creeds. Although these opposing systems had been exclusive and inflexible at the outset, they later accommodated themselves to changing conditions by adopting a pragmatic outlook, which in turn led in the modern period to an extension of the limits of mutual recognition. The Ottoman Empire's continued engagement with European powers resulted

---

[65] Karaosmanoğlu, A. L. (1993). "Officers: Westernization and Democracy." In M. Heper, A. Öncü, and H. Kramer (eds.), *Turkey and the West: Changing Political and Cultural Identities*, pp. 22–28. London and New York: I.B. Tauris. Also see Karal, E. Z. (1988). *Selim III'ün Hatt-ı Hümayunları, 1789–1807*, p. 31; Ankara: Türk Tarih Kurumu; Gat, A. (1989). *The Origins of Military Thought from the Enlightenment to Clausewitz*, pp. 13–24, 28, 59, 187. Oxford: Clarendon Press; and *Atatürk'ün Söylev ve Demeçleri*, vol. 2 (1959), 215, cited in Mardin, S. (1981). "Atatürk and Positivist Thought." In *Atatürk and Turkey of the Republican Era*, p. 60. Ankara: Turkish Union of Chambers.

in its adopting Western diplomatic practices, with the balance of power becoming a central aspect of its diplomacy. However, the Ottoman state was never fully integrated into the European system. Still, the combination of Ottoman statecraft's traditional realism and the prolonged process of Westernization brought a significant internationalist dimension to Turkish officers' foreign policy approach. This shift contributed to a moderating and secularizing influence on nationalism.[66] Mustafa Kemal and his followers, without the burden of a colonial past, did not attribute Turkey's underdevelopment to Western powers. Even during the War of Independence, they did not adopt a broadly antagonistic attitude toward the West. While they criticized the imperialistic actions of some Western nations, they continued to view the West as a primary source of inspiration. Their ultimate aim was to incorporate the Turkish people into the Western community of nations. In their perspective, "there was only one civilization, the Western one, and they would join it despite the West."[67]

On the other hand, Atatürk and Turkish officers were careful not to indulge in illusions about the realities of the international system. The Republican principle of "peace at home, peace abroad" advocated for a policy centered on maintaining the status quo and ensuring the survival of a relatively homogenous nation-state with a distinct Turkish identity. However, this was to be achieved in a Machiavellian world of power politics. Western states, too, operated in the same international system, and their being civilized and progressive did not render them immune to the dictates of power politics. As General Kazım Karabekir, a leading general of the War of Independence, said, "The members of the civilized world are not full of sympathy towards each other. On the contrary, a civilized nation, if it has the capability, would not hesitate to destroy another nation in order to further its national interest."[68]

---

[66] Rustow, D.A. (1958). "Foreign Policy of the Turkish Republic." In C. Roy and Macridis (eds.), *Foreign Policy in World Politics*, p. 313. Englewood Cliffs, NJ: Prentice Hall.

[67] Vali, F. A. (1971). *Bridge across the Bosporus: The Foreign Policy of Turkey*, p. 56. Baltimore and London: The Johns Hopkins University Press. Also see Karaosmanoğlu, A. L. (1993). "Officers: Westernization and Democracy." In M. Heper, A. Öncü, and H. Kramer (eds.), *Turkey and the West: Changing Political and Cultural Identities*, pp. 29–30. London and New York: I.B. Tauris.

[68] Karabekir, K. (1969). İstiklal Harbimiz, p. 170. İstanbul: Türkiye Yayınevi.

It is important to note that, at times, the Turkish officers' interpretation of history extended beyond realpolitik and adopted a perspective that framed the world as a Christian versus Turkish (Muslim) conflict. They believed that a persistent European bias against the Turk existed. On occasion, the Turkish War of Independence was viewed as a modern continuation of the centuries-old struggle against the Crusaders. Such a viewpoint, whose counterparts can be found among Western peoples, continued complicating Turkish officers' conception of the West.[69]

After Turkey joined NATO, many of the country's officers either visited or served at various NATO headquarters. Moreover, many of them attended courses in military schools in the United States. They participated in meetings with allies. These experiences contributed to bridging the psychological gaps with the West. However, it is difficult to say that they eliminated their lack of confidence in their Western counterparts altogether. For the Turkish officer, NATO is seen as highly beneficial for Turkey's security, and vice-versa. The Turkish officer's approach to NATO, however, is mainly national. He is well aware that the security interests of his country do not always align with those of the Alliance.

Let me return to the influence of Clausewitz's ideas and Goltz Pasha's classical, well-established ideas, which do not always conform with those of Clausewitz. Interpretations of Clausewitz reached the Ottoman Empire and the Turkish Republic through the military schools and reforms advised by Helmut von Moltke and von der Goltz Pasha. In particular, Goltz's general staff officer education was one of the most important services to the Ottoman Army. Although Goltz Pasha had a special interest in Clausewitz he mentioned his views many times. But, despite this interest, he refrained from the philosophical approaches and analyses of Clausewitz. In other words, German militarism had overshadowed Clausewitz's approaches and ideas. Colmar von der Goltz was a leading German militarist. Contrary to the Prussian General, he believed military power comes before policy. War and its responsibility must remain with the military commanders.

---

[69] Göksel, B. (1983). *Hatıra ve Misalleriyle Askeri Tarih'in Milli Eğitim ve Kültürdeki Yeri ve Önemi*, p. 7. Ankara: Genelkurmay Başkanlığı.

In his famous book *Millet-i Müselleha (Ordu Millet)*, Goltz Pasha wrote many times about Clausewitz's ideas.[70] In these references, we may read a deep respect and admiration. However, we can see that the Prussian General's philosophical aspect is again forgotten. But, at least, we often hear Clausewitz's name and find the opportunity to get familiar with some of his tactical and operational manœuvres. In *Millet-i Müselleha (Das Volk in Waffen)*, there were quite a number of words, sentences, and paragraphs that would be accepted without hesitation by Clausewitz and von der Goltz (For instance: fog of war, friction, war as commerce, and war of all economic circumstances). We can never have reliable knowledge about the end of war, nor can we fully control its transitory aspects.

Towards the end of the nineteenth century, all military schools and academies, based on *Millet-i Müselleha*, clearly showed that Mustafa Kemal and all the leading commanders of the Turkish War of Independence had a good knowledge of Clausewitz and von der Goltz. However, this acquaintance did not turn into a great and continual interest. During that period, there were two reasons for this lack of success: One was the conflict between Gazi Osman Paşa and a considerable number of officers who wanted high mathematics and high physics to remain in the curriculum. They believed in the significance of the positive sciences for the army and Turkey's modernization. Moreover, Ottoman statecraft had charged the armed forces with guarding modernization. However, the problem extended beyond military reform and modernization alone. The most important problem was to understand the Europe of the subsequent Enlightenment and to transfer the correct knowledge to Turkey. It was not possible to correctly understand the reforms in Europe, Clausewitz's strategic theory, and its philosophical foundation. Such a reform based on Enlightenment would again become misleading unless the Counter-Enlightenment is treated in the same circumstance. Ottoman reform continued with these fluctuations in the Republic. This reform put politics under the authority of the military and removed the reformers from

---

[70] von der Goltz, C. (2016). *Millet'i Müselleha (Ordu Millet—Das Volk in Waffen)*, prepared for publication by Sarıbal, I. (2016) and translated into Turkish by Mehmet Tahir Bey in 1887. During the 1870s, Colmar von der Goltz began drafting and discussing his book, especially in his own country and France. Shortly thereafter, these works reached the Ottoman Empire's administrative, political sections, and military units.

Clausewitz.[71] We can say that Goltz Pasha has accepted one of Clausewitz's definitions of war: war is to make the enemy military power ineffective and to enforce one's will on the opposing side. However, since he does not consider this definition within a dialectical framework, unlike Clausewitz, he does not want to accept that war is akin to "commerce." He emphasizes that he does not "agree" with Clausewitz and "never gave importance to those commanders-in-chief who held the idea of conquering the enemy without shedding blood."[72]

It is worth mentioning one more important point: Goltz Pasha was "in agreement" with Clausewitz. Clausewitz, his mentor General Gerhard von Scharnhorst, and his friend Neidhardt von Gneisenau were the pioneers of the innovative military reform movement in Prussia. The greatest obstacle to reform was the common solidarity and privileged position of aristocratic families within the army, at home, and throughout Europe. In order to build a patriotic and national armed forces, aristocratic solidarity had to be weakened, and privileges had to be abolished. The reformers worked hard and struggled to realize this goal. They tried hard to convince the King, however, they did not succeed. Thanks to the mutual softness of the King and Scharnhorst, the matter was settled by compromise. Some reforms were made, but class privileges were not completely eliminated.[73]

---

[71] Ibid., pp. 97, 189, 183, 193, 275. See also on Colmar von der Goltz: Karaosmanoğlu, A. L. (2021). "Strateji Düşüncesinde Yorum ve Tahrifat: Clausewitz Olayı." In M. Uyar (ed), *Savaş Çalışmaları*, pp. 263–268. İstanbul: Kronik Yayınevi; von der Goltz (2012). In F. Yılmaz, *Yirminci Yüzyıl Başlarında Osmanlı-Alman İlişkileri*. İstanbul: İz Yayıncılık. Additionally, see Yalçınkaya H. and Karadağ, H. (2020). "Türkiye Askeri Yüksek Öğretimine Strateji ve Güvenlik Çalışmalarındaki Değişimin Yansımaları: Kara Harp Okulu Örneği." In A. Karaosmanoğlu, and E. Aydınlı (eds.), *Strateji Düşüncesi*, pp. 313–334. İstanbul: Bilgi Üniversitesi Yayınları.

[72] Karaosmanoğlu, A. L. (2021). "Strateji Düşüncesinde Yorum ve Tahrifat: Clausewitz Olayı." In M. Uyar, *Savaş Çalışmaları*, pp. 63–75. İstanbul: Kronik Yayınevi; Daase, C., and Davis, J. (eds.) (2015), *Clausewitz and Small War*. Oxford: Oxford University Press; and Scheipers S. (2018). *On Small War: Carl von Clausewitz and People's War*. Oxford: Oxford University Press.

[73] Paret, P. (2009). *The Cognitive Challenge of War: Prussia 1806*, pp. 72–103. Princeton and Oxford: Princeton University Press.

Goltz Pasha devoted the first and second parts of his book[74] to the organization and personnel of the army (eight chapters in total). From Pasha's texts, it is understood that the military privileges of noble families were weakened, and merit began to come to the fore. While higher education and science became essential for the *Heyet- i Zabitan*, it was also necessary to give importance to manners and morals. Young people who possess, or are ready to possess, these qualities are now coming not only from the upper classes but also from bourgeois families. The army will also have to adapt itself to this social change.

Goltz Pasha uses Clausewitz's concepts of "genius" and "will" or "high will" by quoting the Prussian General in the second part, the first chapter of his book, under the title *Usul-i Sevk ve Tahriki: Command*. He cites Clausewitz: "Strength of heart does not only consist in generating violent excitement but also in maintaining equanimity of feeling during the most violent excitement... [and] in preserving and proving the power of thought and reflection"[75] The fact that *Milleti-i Müselleha* was translated from German into Ottoman shortly after the end of the nineteenth century and that von der Goltz Pasha served as a lecturer at the Ottoman Military Schools and Military Academy clearly shows that the officers commanding the War of Independence, especially Mustafa Kemal, were familiar with Clausewitz. However, it is not possible to say that this familiarity turned into a great interest. In general, the impact of both of Goltz's missions was significant. At Goltz's suggestion, applied military courses were added to the academic curriculum in 1884. Nevertheless, purely military courses remained limited. Gazi Osman Pasha and the professors at Harbiye could not be convinced. For example, in their view, it was crucial that higher mathematics and physics remained in the curriculum. For them, positive sciences were essential for Ottoman modernization and reforms. It was not only about military reform. It was about understanding Europe after the Enlightenment and transferring it to the country.

---

[74] von Der Goltz, C. (2012). "Yirminci Yüzyıl Başlarında Osmanlı-Alman İlişkileri." In F. Yılmaz (ed.), *Golç Paşa'nın Hatıratı*. İstanbul: İz Yayıncılık.

[75] von Der Goltz, C. (2012). "Yirminci Yüzyıl Başlarında Osmanlı-Alman İlişkileri." In F. Yılmaz (ed.), *Golç Paşa'nın Hatıratı*, İstanbul: İz Yayıncılık.

However, it was also clear that reformism was based solely on the Enlightenment without understanding the philosophical basis of European reforms. Clausewitz's theory of strategy would remain baseless and incomplete. Unfortunately, even if the Ottoman Military Staff had benefited from Goltz Pasha's book and lectures, it would not have been possible for them to research Clausewitz. Another aspect that reinforced this negativity was that The Ottoman Palace appointed the modernized military as the chief guardian of the modernization process. This aspect of Ottoman modernization continued in Republican Turkey for 2000 years. This assignment, of course, placed politics under the dominance of military power and was a far cry from Clausewitz.[76]

---

[76] von Der Goltz, C. (2012). "Yirminci Yüzyıl Başlarında Osmanlı-Alman İlişkileri." In F. Yılmaz (ed.), *Golç Paşa'nın Hatıratı*, p. 81. İstanbul: İz Yayıncılık; Uyar, M., and Erickson, E. J. (2009). *A Military History of the Ottomans: From Osman to Atatürk*, p. 18. Oxford: Oxford University Press. For a detailed account, see Özcan, G., (2020). "Türkiye'de Milli Güvenlik Kavramının Gelişimi ve Ulusal Strateji Arayışları." In A. L. Karaosmanoğlu, and E. Aydınlı (eds.). *Strateji Düşüncesi: Kuram, Paradoks ve Uygulama*, pp. 123–144. İstanbul: Bilgi Üniversitesi Yayınları.

The Cold War and Post-Cold War Era

4.1. The Transformation of Civil–Military Relations in Republican Turkey: Spaces of Common Understanding and Democratization

At this point of our study, I would like to share a talk I presented at the International Political Science Association (IPSA) Congress in Santiago, Chile, on July 12–16, 2009. The talk was about *The Transformation of Civil–Military Relations: The Spaces of Common Understanding and Democratization in Republican Turkey.* I also wrote an article based on that talk, which was in *Turkish Studies.*[77] Although the text was not identical to the Santiago presentation, it was a good reflection of the subject-matter. The following section contains a similar subject-matter.

One of the major challenges to Turkey's ongoing democratic consolidation has been the significant influence of the armed forces on public affairs. This issue has acquired ever-increasing internal and international significance since the country's transition to a multi-party system in the mid-1940s. The political role of the Turkish Armed Forces (TAF) has complicated democratic processes by restricting the authority of elected civilian governments. The military assumed control of the government three times—in 1960, 1971, and 1980—and forced its resignation in 1997. Additionally, since 1950, there have been multiple attempts by certain factions within the military to overthrow

---

[77] *Turkish Studies*, 12 (2), June 2011, 253–264

democratically elected governments, though the watchful oversight of senior officers thwarted these efforts.

Civil–military relations became a key international issue with Turkey's application for European Union (EU) membership. Despite some setbacks, Turkey has made significant progress in establishing more democratic civil–military relations. Between 2002 and 2005, in an effort to meet the Copenhagen criteria for EU membership, the Turkish parliament amended the Constitution several times. It passed new laws to limit the military's influence over matters that should primarily fall under the responsibility of elected civilian officials. While these reforms aligned Turkey more closely with democratic norms, the military's political influence remained evident. In 2006 and 2007, military leaders' public statements underscored the armed forces' ongoing power in public affairs. A particularly striking example of this occurred on April 27, 2007, when the military issued an "electronic ultimatum" during the presidential election, highlighting the persistent political role of the TAF.

Since this electronic ultimatum from the General Staff and its prompt and decisive refutation by the government in April 2007, Turkey's civil–military relations have taken a perplexing turn toward further democratization. Many, both domestically and internationally, including sharp analysts, anticipated that the confrontation would either lead to a coup d'état or, at the very least, provoke significant military interference in politics. Surprisingly, neither of these occurred. Instead, a new pattern emerged, characterized by mutual understanding and a subtle yet effective collaboration between the civilian government and the military. It was hard to imagine that a prime minister with Islamic roots and the secularist generals would meet almost weekly in addition to their regular official meetings. What once seemed clear turned out to be far from it. This unexpected proximity presented a "disturbing puzzle." What could explain this new and perplexing development?

Analysts discussing civil–military relations in Turkey often present a dichotomy between the secular, patriotic, rational, and modern soldier and the elected politician, who is viewed as inefficient and anti-secular. This framework has frequently been used to justify military takeovers and other forms of military involvement in politics.[78] Critics of the military's influence often

---

[78] Jenkins, G. (2001). *Context and Circumstance: The Turkish Military and Politics*, Adelphi Paper 337, pp. 15, 21. Oxford: Oxford University Press/IISS.

rely on a similar binary, highlighting the conflictual nature of the relationship between the military and the civilian elite. They view civil–military matters as "power relations involving constant confrontation and tension."[79] It is also argued that civilian politicians often acquiesce to the military's demands and "even seek an expanded role for the military."[80] According to this perspective, the problem goes beyond simply implementing democratic control over the armed forces; it extends to civilian empowerment, which involves enabling civilian governments to assert control not only over the military but also over the country's broader political, economic, and institutional life[81]—domains which the military tends to dominate by its very nature. Some scholars take this argument further, claiming that the TAF tendency to "make and break governments" is not a transient issue.[82] The military has primarily maintained and expanded its political influence by placing excessive emphasis on internal security issues, such as "Islamic activism and Kurdish nationalism," rather than focusing on external threats.[83]

However, such confrontational arguments have not been universally accepted by all scholars and analysts. As early as 2005, a report from the Centre for European Security Studies (CESS) challenged the widespread European view of the Turkish military's political role, describing it as exaggerated and overly simplistic. The report specifically criticized the notion that the TAF was "a state within a state for all practical purposes." It argued

---

[79] Demirel, T. (January 2004). "Soldiers and Civilians: The Dilemma of Turkish Democracy," *Middle Eastern Studies* 40 (1), 145.

[80] Demirel, T. (January 2004). "Soldiers and Civilians: The Dilemma of Turkish Democracy," *Middle Eastern Studies*, 40 (1), 128.

[81] Cizre Ü. (2004). "Democratic Control of Armed Forces on the Edge of Europe: The Case of Turkey." In H. Born, K. Haltiner, and M. Malesic (eds.), *Renaissance of Democratic Control of Armed Forces in Contemporary Societies*, p. 113. Baden-Baden: Nomos Verlag.

[82] Cizre, Ü, (2004). "Democratic Control of Armed Forces on the Edge of Europe: The Case of Turkey." In H. Born, K. Haltiner, and M. Malesic (eds.), *Renaissance of Democratic Control of Armed Forces in Contemporary Societies*, p. 110. Baden-Baden: Nomos Verlag. For the role of the military in "securitization," see also Kirişçi, K. (September 2006). *Turkey's Foreign Policy in Turbulent Times*, Chaillot Paper no. 92, pp. 32–38. Paris: Institute for Security Studies.

[83] Cizre, Ü. (2004). "Democratic Control of Armed Forces on the Edge of Europe: The Case of Turkey." In H. Born, K. Haltiner, and M. Malesic (eds.), *Renaissance of Democratic Control of Armed Forces in Contemporary Societies*, p. 104. Baden-Baden: Nomos Verlag.

that this portrayal was "a caricature of present-day Turkey," one that was not only unflattering but also increasingly inaccurate.[84]

Karabekir Akkoyunlu argues that it is inaccurate to view Turkish democratization in terms of a simple binary, pitting an authoritarian military against civilian politicians who favor democracy. Instead, he suggests that Turkish democratization should be examined through a comprehensive approach that looks at the development of democratic political culture in the country.[85]

While dichotomous and confrontational analyses have historically reflected certain aspects of the Turkish case, their explanatory power is diminishing due to several new and evolving trends. My main contention is that binary approaches, though scholarly, often fail to account for the highly interactive and transformative nature of civil–military relations. These approaches tend to downplay the potential for collaboration and institutional interpenetration within the broader context of shared understandings in Turkey's historical and political landscape.[86] Civil authorities depend on the armed forces to safeguard the state's defense and maintain the country's territorial integrity. In return, the armed forces depend on the civil authority to legitimize their actions following core democratic values.[87] Thus, the core issue is not merely about maximizing civilian control over the military; the real challenge lies in "maintaining a strong and effective military that poses no threat to the civilian elite."[88] This issue can be effectively addressed by promoting a collaborative

---

[84] Wim van Eekelen (chairman) and David Greenwood (rapporteur), (November 2005). *Turkish Civil-Military Relations and the EU: Preparation for Continuing Convergence, Final Report of a Task Force*, p. 12. Groningen: CESS.

[85] Akkoyunlu, K. (2007). *Military Reform and Democratisation: Turkish and Indonesian Experiences at the Turn of the Millennium*, Adelphi Paper no. 392, p. 36. London: Routledge/IISS.

[86] Mardin, S. (June 2005). "Turkish Islamic Exceptionalism Yesterday and Today: Continuity, Rupture and Reconstruction in Operational Codes," *Turkish Studies* 6 (2), 146.

[87] Bland, D. L. "Your Obedient Servant: The Military's Role in the Civil Control of Armed Forces." In H. Born, K. Haltiner, and M. Malesic (eds.), *Renaissance of Democratic Control of Armed Forces in Contemporary Societies*, p. 25.

[88] Burk, J. (2002). "Theories of Democratic Civil-Military Relations," *Armed Forces & Society* 29 (1 Fall), 15.

relationship between military and civilian elites.[89] Ultimately, the successful oversight of the military relies on the cooperation between the officer corps and the civilian government. Both are interconnected within the same state framework and depend on each other.

Given the unique organizational and functional characteristics of the military institution and the increasing overlap of internal and external security concerns in today's world, no civilian authority can ignore the growing significance of military input in political decision-making. This issue has gained notable attention recently, especially in countries like Great Britain and the United States, due to the "war on terror" and the invasion of Iraq. General Sir Richard Dannett's condemnation of his government's choice to invade Iraq was an exceptional instance of defiance from a sitting army chief in a liberal democracy such as the United Kingdom. However, this event stresses the need for a revised approach to civil–military relations. Sir Richard's concerns also reflected the dissatisfaction within the military in the United States.[90] In the same year, Hew Strachan published an article in *Survival*, criticizing perspectives that treat the armed forces merely as a tool of the civilian government without acknowledging the nature of that tool. He emphasized the importance of "dialogue between politicians and soldiers" and the need to "harmonize the two elements."[91] He further proposed: "The principle we need to adopt is civil–military integration, based on the concepts

---

[89] Burk, J. (2002). "Theories of Democratic Civil-Military Relations," *Armed Forces & Society* 29 (1 Fall) 17. For contemporary theory, see also Feaver, P. D. (1996). "The Civil-Military Problematique: Huntington, Janowitz, and the Question of Civilian Control," *Armed Forces & Society* 23 (2 Winter), 149–178; Bland, D. L. (2001). "Patterns in Liberal Democratic Civil-Military Relations," *Armed Forces & Society* 27 (4 Summer) 525–540; Cottey, A., Edmunds, T., and Forster, A. (2002). "The Second Generation Problematique: Rethinking Democracy and Civil-Military Relations," *Armed Forces & Society* 29 (1 Fall), 31–56; and Schiff, R. L. (1995). "Civil-Military Relations Reconsidered: A Theory of Concordance," *Armed Forces & Society*, 22 (1 Fall), 7–24.

[90] *Financial Times*, October 14–15, 2006, 1–2, 6; and *The Guardian*, October 18, 2006, 1. For the civil-military tension in the United States, see Desch, M. C. (2007). "Bush and the Generals," *Foreign Affairs* 86 (3) (May/June), 97–108.

[91] Strachan, H. (2006). "Making Strategy: Civil-Military Relations after Iraq," *Survival* 48 (3) (Autumn), 67.

of equality in counsel and the harmonization of effects."[92] According to Hew Strachan, this revised framework for civil–military relations would reintegrate both the armed forces and the government within the state structure, making parliamentary oversight of both the civilian and military branches of the executive more effective. As a result, it would enhance the smooth operation of the democratic system,[93] with the final authority resting with the civilian leadership.

In today's world, the political and military realms are increasingly intertwined. Civil–military relations should be considered neither conflictual nor hierarchical. Political and military leaders should work together to establish a constructive consensus, addressing not only defense and security policies but also the governance of their relationship within the state and society. These ongoing discussions in liberal democracies such as the United States and Great Britain are equally relevant for a country like Turkey, which is working to strengthen its democracy amid a complex and challenging security environment. In the first view, the civil–military problem in liberal democracies may seem different from the situation in unconsolidated democratic regimes, where the military often displays an undemocratic habit of interfering with political processes. In both cases, the most politically suitable solution depends on establishing a balanced and cooperative relationship between the democratically elected civilian government and the military while ensuring that ultimate authority rests with the former.

The confrontational approach to the Turkish case emphasizes internal political factors while overlooking the broader security context and international influences. On the one hand, growing ethnic separatism, coupled with regional security challenges involving external forces and the growth of democratic and liberal values due to globalization, has blurred the demarcation line between the internal and the international. This development has undermined the internal dimension of security challenges, making both military and civilian perspectives increasingly externally oriented. Moreover,

---

[92] Strachan, H. (2006). "Making Strategy: Civil-Military Relations after Iraq," *Survival* 48 (3) (Autumn), 76.
[93] Strachan, H. (2006). "Making Strategy: Civil-Military Relations after Iraq," *Survival* 48 (3) (Autumn), 79–80.

today, we witness an "aggregation of different conflicts"[94] in the Middle East. The convergence of different security challenges from both internal and external sources has brought the political and other non-military aspects of conflicts to the forefront.

The conflict-oriented discourse overlooks the historical and cultural context by simplifying the complexities of Ottoman-Turkish modernization into a binary opposition. However, civil–military relations, like any social or individual relationship, unfold within cultural patterns, which are "historically created systems of meaning in terms of which we give form, order, point, and direction to our lives."[95] A key aspect of Ottoman-Turkish political culture has been "the interactive or dialogical dimension" of "the clashes between alternative frameworks of meaning," in which "the two horizons fused together."[96] This potential for a dialogical process has remained embedded in the very structure of the state under the Republic. Şerif Mardin offers a compelling insight into this phenomenon, stating that the history of modern Turkey should not be seen merely as a conflict between republicanism and Sultanism or as a struggle between Islam and secularism. Instead, it is a complex interaction between traditional forces and modernity, where these forces have influenced each other and evolved due to their proximity. It is also a narrative of how new spaces emerged where these forces intersected and transformed.[97]

The interaction between these forces has legitimized change and facilitated their adaptation to modernity.[98] The state played a central role in creating shared spaces of understanding designed to ensure its survival by adjusting to evolving circumstances. Throughout this ongoing process, despite occasional disruptions, there have been extended periods in the history of the

---

[94] Strachan, H. (February–March 2008). "Strategy and the Limitation of War," *Survival* 50 (1), 34.

[95] Geertz, C. (1973). *The Interpretation of Cultures*, p. 52. New York: Basic Books.

[96] Outwaite, W. (1994). "Hans-Georg Gadamer." In Q. Skinner (ed.), *The Return of Grand Theory in the Human Sciences*, p. 34. Cambridge: Cambridge University Press.

[97] Mardin, Ş. (2005). "Turkish Islamic Exceptionalism Yesterday and Today: Continuity, Rupture and Reconstruction in Operational Codes." *Turkish Studies* 6 (2), 145–165, 160.

[98] Karpat, K. H. (2001). *The Politicization of Islam*, p. 420. Oxford: Oxford University Press.

Turkish Republic where civil–military relations operated within a relatively stable democratic framework. Notable examples include the Turkish War of Independence (1919–1923), Turkey's integration into NATO and the subsequent Democrat Party era (1949–1958), which ended in a military coup in 1960, the Özal period (1983–1993), and the EU reform process from 2002 to 2005. These instances indicate that the collegial relationship between the Justice and Development Party (JDP) and the TAF beginning in the spring of 2007 is not an anomaly but part of a broader historical pattern. The source of the initial perplexity was apparently an interpretive neglect of the historical and cultural context. Suppose civil–military relations are a context-specific cultural and socio-political construction. In that case, we should also address the following questions: How did civil–military relations acquire meaning in different periods (specific contexts), and what implications did this have for political practice? Secondly, is the recent change that began in 2007 ephemeral, or is it irreversible?

In the recent history of the Republic of Turkey, there have been periods when civil–military relations were carried out within an effective democratic framework. A significant development in this direction occurred in the 1980s following the September 12, 1980, military coup. The Motherland Party, which came to power in 1983 under Turgut Özal's leadership, had strong Islamic grassroots support. However, the party pursued policies aimed at integrating with the global economy and shifting the country away from its state-controlled, protectionist economic structure. Özal, a staunch advocate of economic liberalism, emphasized entrepreneurial interests and international interdependence. The shift toward economic liberalization positively impacted the defense industry, encouraging collaboration between the public and private sectors. Expanding business ties between the TAF and private enterprises, both domestic and international, contributed to moderating the military's traditionally state-centric stance on internal and international affairs. This new policy also facilitated foreign investment and technological advancements in the defense sector. To further this transformation, the government created the Defense Industry Development and Support Administration (DIDA), later renamed the Undersecretariat of Defense Industries, to enhance cross-sector cooperation and promote the transfer of technology and capital to Turkey. Additionally, DIDA managed the Defense Industry Support Fund, which was financed through indirect taxes on luxury imports. This fund played a key role in supporting the defense industry and financing joint projects, the most notable being the F-16 production initiative led by the newly established Turkish Aerospace Industries (TAI).[99]

Turgut Özal's strong interest in security and defense, coupled with his efforts to accelerate the development of the defense industry, fostered a significant area of mutual understanding and coordinated action between the democratically elected civilian government and the military. This cooperative relationship with the TAF reinforced political authority and enabled a smooth yet swift civilianization of the political system following the 1980 military coup.[100] Özal played a decisive role in shaping security and defense policy, successfully asserting his political influence over the TAF, as seen in his appointment of General Necip Torumtay as Chief of General Staff in 1986. Additionally, political and economic liberalization paved the way for Turkey's accession to the European Customs Union (ECU) in 1995 and its formal EU candidacy in 1999.

Turgut Özal was firmly committed to the supremacy of civilian authority over the military and took significant steps to uphold this principle throughout his presidency. A notable instance occurred during the Gulf crisis in December 1990, when a considerable divergence of views emerged between President Özal and the Chief of General Staff, General Necip Torumtay. As a result, General Torumtay resigned from his post. In his public statement, General Torumtay explained his resignation by emphasizing the differences in perspective between him and the president regarding Turkey's stance on the Gulf crisis:

> There is no conflict between the military and civilian officials. The Turkish Armed Forces commanders know very well that the civilian authority always has the final word. The army knows where it stands... Of course, in meetings with civilian officials, differences of opinion will arise. But this is only to be expected.[101]

---

[99] Karaosmanoğlu, A. L., and Kibaroğlu, M. (2002). "Defense Reform in Turkey." In I. Gyarmati, and T. Winkler (eds.), *Post-Cold War Defense Reform: Lessons Learned in Europe and the United States*, pp. 157–159. Washington, DC: Brassey's.

[100] Kuloğlu, A., and Sahin, M. (2006). "The Past and the Future of Civil-Military Relations in Turkey." In S. Faltas, and S. Jansen (eds). *Governance and the Military: Perspectives for Change in Turkey*, Harmonie Paper, pp. 96–97. Groningen: CESS.

[101] Dateline (15 December 1990), p. 2.

Another significant period of civil–military reconciliation based on demo-cratic principles occurred under the governance of the JDP. While the JDP's founders had strong Islamist roots, they followed in the footsteps of Turgut Özal, notably moving away from religious militancy. Instead, they adopted a more harmonized position with the global economic system and the EU. This shift facilitated improved civil–military relations, with the military playing a less dominant role in politics compared to previous periods, as the JDP pursued integration with international markets and democratic reforms.

Additionally, the JDP government placed significant emphasis on active policies not only in neighboring regions but also within NATO and peace operations. Turkey's participation in peace operations has played a key role in transforming the Turkish military, aligning it with emerging security concepts prioritizing human and societal security dimensions.[102] By the twenty-first century, the military became more cautious about involving itself too overtly in politics, establishing a kind of modus vivendi with the civilian government.[103] Several factors contribute to this trend. First, in the contemporary era, democracy is closely tied to modernization, which neces-sitates civilian primacy. As the "agent of modernization," the military has become increasingly aware of this historical shift since the end of World War II. Second, the military acknowledges that political involvement com-promises the professionalism of its officer corps. Finally, growing pressure from public opinion for greater democratization has made military-political statements more contentious. Statements made by the Chief of Staff and Force Commanders frequently ignite intense media discussions, with many columnists and academics criticizing such interventions as unjustifiable interference in public affairs.

The TAF backed JDP's efforts toward EU membership, as well as the associated reforms and the significant shift in Cyprus policy. In June 2006, Foreign Minister Abdullah Gül accredited the military's important role in supporting Turkey's EU-related objectives and reforms. He stated that

---

[102] Oğuzlu, H. T., and Güngör, U. (December 2006). "Peace Operations and the Transformation of Turkey's Security Policy," *Contemporary Security Policy* 27 (3), 472–488.
[103] Heper, M., and Itzkowitz-Shifrinson, J. R. (2005). "Civil-Military Relations in Israel and Turkey," *Journal of Political and Military Sociology*, 33 (2) (Winter), 244.

the reforms would have been significantly harder to implement without the military's support, as they understand Turkey's interests and possess a long-term strategic vision. He added that the shift in Turkey's Cyprus policy was made possible by their active involvement, and there has been ongoing communication with them.[104]

Although these reforms and public demands for further democratization moved Turkey closer to democratic standards, military leaders occasionally made public statements in 2006 and 2007 that reflected the armed forces' ongoing political influence. A clear instance occurred on April 27, 2007, when the military issued an "electronic memorandum" to interfere in the presidential election. However, this intervention proved ineffective, as the JDP achieved a decisive electoral victory in July 2007.

By May 2007, even before the events later that year, civil–military relations in Turkey had shifted noticeably. The military's cautious and distant stance became more apparent, and a new pattern of collaboration emerged. This new dynamic involved close and effective cooperation between the civilian government and the military, particularly regarding the Kurdish issue in general and efforts to combat the *Partiya Karkeran Kurdistan* (PKK) specifically. Recently, the air and land forces carried out fifteen cross-border operations targeting PKK positions in northern Iraq. Ahead of these operations, the government made significant diplomatic efforts to secure political support from the United States, Europe, and the Middle East.

Since then, Prime Minister Erdoğan and the Chief of Staff have held nearly weekly meetings, formally and informally, to assess the operations and address broader security concerns. In a statement released after one such meeting in early June 2007, officials highlighted that the fight against terrorism would continue "on the basis of democracy and rule of law." They noted the existence of "full harmony and coordination" between the civilian government and the military.[105]

This cooperative relationship not only opened the door for potential democratic progress but also emphasized the significance of the strategic interaction between political decision-making and military actions. Moreover,

---

[104] Reported by Yetkin, M. (June 15, 2006). "Gül: Askerlerin AB Desteğinden Memnunuz" [Gül: We are Happy with the Military's Support to the EU Project], *Radikal*, p. 6.

[105] Briefing (18 June 2007), 6.

it emphasized the inherently political nature of counter-terrorism efforts and the Kurdish issue. Two primary factors drove this collaboration: first, the need to preserve national unity, which became a top priority before and during the operations, as the military sought to avoid any actions that might divide the nation. Secondly, and perhaps more importantly, there has been a notable shift in the approach to combating the PKK. The partial internationalization of the PKK issue and the broader Kurdish question, along with their intersection with the ongoing complex conflict in Iraq, has created a set of interrelated security challenges originating both domestically and internationally. As a result, the political and other non-military aspects of the issue have become more prominent. Furthermore, the resurgence of PKK activity, despite the military's success in the 1990s, has reinforced the importance of adopting a more comprehensive strategy—one that goes beyond military operations. This new approach involves coordinating military and political efforts with measures that address economic, diplomatic, socio-psychological, and public relations dimensions.[106] Achieving this goal naturally necessitates close collaboration between civilian authorities and the military. However, despite the ongoing cooperation between these two sides, there is still no clear indication that this new perspective has yet been translated into a fully developed, comprehensive strategy.

To sum up, binary and confrontational analyses are inadequate to understand and explain civil–military relations in Turkey. Ottoman-Turkish modernization relied on the state's efforts to establish spaces for shared understanding, where interactions between traditional and modern forces took place, leading to significant transformations. These interactions provided legitimacy for change and supported the adaptation of state institutions to both modernity and the evolving environment. I suggest that the development of civil–military relations in Turkey can only be understood from this historical-cultural perspective. However, any relationship that is understandable through this approach should also be open to causal explanation, which

---

[106] For the emphasis placed on the non-military aspects of security, see the Opening Address of the International Symposium by the Commander of Turkish Armed Forces, General Yaşar Büyükanit (Istanbul, 31 May 2007); and the Opening Address of the Academic Year 2007–2008 of the War College by the Turkish Land Forces Commander, General İlker Başbuğ (Ankara, 24 September 2007).

would attribute additional meaning to the relationship. Throughout the history of civil–military relations in the Republic, there have been extended periods of cooperation where the civilian political authority held the initiative and the final decision, despite occasional disruptions. Civilian politicians and the military were not always in conflict. The contention was to clarify this historical fact and to answer the question of what motivated them to come together and collaborate.

As Turkey continues to integrate into a globalizing world and participates in organizations like NATO and the OSCE while pursuing EU membership, the intersubjective relationship extends beyond the domestic sphere. The involvement of external actors becomes inevitable, expanding the cultural framework within which this dialogical process unfolds. The contemporary international context, which increasingly overlaps with domestic dynamics, is a deterrent to overt military intervention in politics. The way Turkey dealt with the Kurdish problem and the PKK from 1985 to 2006 created a gulf between policy and military practice. The governments had left the responsibility of dealing with these issues almost completely to the armed forces. Since then, the civilian government and the General Staff have increasingly become aware of the need to change the flawed understanding of the nature of these security challenges. The repeated resurgence of the PKK and the persistence of the Kurdish issue, despite past military successes, demonstrated the need to reassess military measures within a broader, more comprehensive strategy. This strategy would integrate military efforts with political and other non-military initiatives. Such an approach would require close cooperation between the military and the democratically elected civilian government. Additionally, the growing international attention to the Kurdish issue has heightened the importance of maintaining legitimacy in domestic decision-making processes. This development has also prompted greater political involvement and fostered a more collaborative relationship between the military and the government.

Internal and international developments have considerably diminished the military's political power, pushing civil–military relations in Turkey toward greater civilian political initiative and reduced military influence in public affairs. Achieving consensus among political parties on creating a more democratic sense of balance between secularism and religion, as well as addressing the Kurdish issue within the context of the unitary state, would likely speed up the move toward greater democratic control over the military. While some progress has been made in civilian control of the armed forces, Turkey still falls short of EU standards as of 2024.

4.2. Nuclear Strategy and Turkey in the Cold War

After Turkey became a member of NATO in 1952, the German-Prussian influence on the armed forces gradually dissolved. We know that during the Korean War, difficulties arose over the different training manuals and command and control relations. Following 1952, the U.S. armed forces began to adopt and translate U.S. military terms and regulations. However, a century and a half of German-Prussian influence did not become completely invisible in a short period. Both influences continued in the form of dualism without creating a synthesis. A recent article deals with this problem in detail. Within the framework of U.S. military aid and the advisors sent, there is no doubt that a certain atmosphere of cooperation was created, albeit not complete. As stated in the Güvenç and Uyar study cited above, an intense atmosphere of solidarity and trust between the two states did not develop. According to the historical data and events analyzed by the authors, the armed forces of both countries had difficulties reconciling from the beginning of military and political cooperation for institutional, strategic, and cultural reasons. U.S. aid to Turkey required a change in military culture and institutions. However, instilling a new culture could not be done in a short period. Therefore, the priority was to complete training with new weapons as soon as possible.[107]

During the Cuban Missile Crisis, Washington's withdrawal of the medium-range, nuclear-tipped Jupiter missiles stationed in Turkey without consulting or even informing the Turkish government was deeply disturbing. It led to a distrust of the super states. Moreover, the Cyprus conflict, which flared up in the 1960s and 1970s, made deepening military cooperation even more difficult. The older generation of Turkish officers had no complaints about the overlap between German and Turkish military culture, excluding Clausewitz. At the same time, interest in Clausewitz was growing in the

---

[107] Güvenç, S., and Uyar, M., (2021). "Lost in Translation or Transformation? The Impact of American Aid on the Turkish Military, 1947–1960," *Cold War History*. <https://doi.org/10.1080/14682745.2020.1866551>.

United States. My greatest interest was studying "nuclear strategy" and "limited war." Bernard Brodie called *On War* the most significant work on war. Herman Kahn, Brodie, and, to some extent, Albert Wohlstetter were inspired by Clausewitz's theory and sought answers to how to deter a possible nuclear war. Robert Osgood developed a new theory of limited war, drawing on Clausewitz's theory. Even their terminology was reminiscent of the Prussian General: massive response, flexible response, and controlled escalation. These studies also revealed various choices between nuclear war and surrender, freeing the parties from choosing between two extreme options. The work of America's Neo-Clausewitzian intellectuals paved the way for the nuclear arms control treaties agreed upon by the two superpowers.

When Turkey became a member of NATO, it authorized the deployment of tactical nuclear weapons in its territory. Nevertheless, it was not even remotely interested in the nuclear strategy work conducted in the United States. However, only a small part of this work and scientific research was kept secret. Most of it was made public through think tank reports and university publications. Unfortunately, Turkey did not benefit from this transparency. The secrecy of our military in those days and the absence of military history and strategy theory courses in the political science departments of our universities left us far away from contemporary adaptations of Clausewitz. The definitions and concepts in Carl von Clausewitz's works remain relevant in the age of nuclear weapons, intercontinental missiles, asymmetric warfare, terrorism, and ever-evolving technology. With its theoretical structure and reasoning, *On War* (Vom Kriege) is not only a book of armaments, battle tactics, *maneuvers*, and strategies but also a logician and resolver of conflicts.[108]

The debate surrounding NATO enlargement has provided limited clarity regarding its potential impact on Europe's southern periphery and nearby regions, such as the Balkans, the Caucasus, the Black Sea, and the eastern Mediterranean—areas that include NATO members Turkey, and Greece. The dissolution of the Soviet Union initially created opportunities for newly independent states to build cooperative relationships with the West and each other. However, from the perspective of Turkey's security policy, unchecked NATO expansion could negatively affect security and stability in these southern

---

[108] Brodie, B. (1973). *War and Politics*, pp. 375–432. London: Cassell.

regions. Moreover, Turkey asserts that neither NATO nor the regional states can effectively promote security and stability without Russia's cooperation. The process of NATO enlargement has set in motion a trajectory with potentially significant and pressing consequences for the Euro-Atlantic area and the southern regions in particular. Despite these concerns, it is now too late to reverse this trend.[109]

4.3. Turkey's Geopolitical and Cultural Priorities: From the Atlantic Alliance (1952) to an Important Step in Democratization (2014)

After the end of the Cold War, Turkey has evolved as a proactive, independent, and assertive actor in three arenas: The Caucasus, the Balkans, and the Middle East. These regions are also centers of strategic interest to great powers, specifically the United States, Europe, and Russia. Thus, it is understandable that changes in the foreign and security policy of a NATO ally with the second-largest military force in the alliance and a growing economy should be of major significance and concern to its adversaries as well as its allies. This section will principally focus on the Middle East, where the developments are much more complex, much less manageable, and much more threatening than in the other two regions. However, we will occasionally reference these to clarify the evolution of positions and behavior of actors for comparative purposes. This section will tackle the following questions within this context: What are the characteristics of Turkey's new foreign and security policy? What are the internal and external drivers of the new policy? How does it affect its relations with its allies and Russia? How do they respond? What are the limits of this policy, and how sustainable is it? How could it develop and change over a longer period, and in which direction?

Turkey has always been strategically important for the defense of Western security interests. In return, as a NATO ally, Turkey's security and defense have enjoyed allied support and assistance. Despite its close cooperation in defense and other matters, its strategic relationship with Western allies has not always been easy. Notwithstanding its NATO obligations, Ankara has

---

[109] Karaosmanoğlu, A. L. (June 1999). "NATO Enlargement and the South: A Turkish Perspective," *Security Dialogue* 30 (2), 213, 221.

maintained a regional perspective on security and other interests. The TAFs have had to make strategic plans to reckon with their capabilities to operate either in tandem with allies or alone. This was the case even during the Cold War. Turkey's posture, however, remained non-interventionist and status quo-oriented until the end of the Cold War.

Before coming back to the radical changes that took place in the post-Cold War era, it would be relevant and useful to say a few more words about the features of the cultural context of Turkey's relations with the West. Turkey holds a complex position in the Western world. As a NATO ally and a member of most Western international institutions, it is politically and ideologically an integral part of the Western community of nations. Turkey's alignment with NATO after WWII cannot be explained solely by the Soviet threat and other strategic considerations; it is also the accomplishment of an aspiration to make the country an equal member of the Western community of nations at a time when the nation was embracing the transition to multiparty democracy. Since then, Turkey's NATO membership and its people's democratic aspirations have remained its most functional bond with the West. On the other hand, Turkey is set apart from the West by quite a number of features, such as its geographic location, social-political evolution, and history. It is a predominantly Muslim country with a unique democratic and secular tradition, though it is still working to resolve some human rights issues.

Given the challenges of transitioning from an Empire to a Republic and Europe's great powers' occupation of its remaining territories after World War I, some lingering mistrust toward Europe was perhaps inevitable. Ankara did not feel secure until it joined the Atlantic Alliance in 1952, and the Cold War temporarily helped resolve previous security concerns. However, this mutual distrust persisted for a long time. It stemmed not only from Turkey's bitter experiences with European powers during the final century of imperial decline but also, perhaps more importantly, from the centuries-old intersubjective process through which Turkish and European identities were shaped. This process can be viewed through a "self and other" dichotomy, contributing to Turkey's relative marginalization within Europe. Elements of this sentiment can still be observed among the European populace. Similarly, despite the long-standing Westernization efforts and Atatürk's reforms, both public opinion and Turkey's foreign and security policy elite continue to express a certain level of discomfort with Europe and, at times, toward the

United States. However, neither the contemporary divide between Islam and the West nor the lingering mistrust between Turkey and Europe has deterred Turkey's commitment to Westernization, which has been a central feature of the nation, alongside its persistent Eastern characteristics. This dichotomy has led to a complex and ambivalent political and strategic approach.

4.4. The Impact of Global Political Trends on Turkey's Security

Globalization in security is often understood as "going beyond the national interdependence security framework."[110] This shift emphasizes multilateral cooperation and a transition from direct confrontations to collaborative approaches.[111] One of the key consequences of globalization is the reinforcement of universal norms and values alongside the defense of a "moral minimum," as seen in cases such as Bosnia and Kosovo. However, globalization also fosters political particularism and exclusivity, exposing the nation-state to challenges from sub-national groups and non-state actors with transnational affiliations. For state elites, these entities often represent centrifugal forces or, at the very least, sources of instability.

Shaped by its historical and geopolitical context, Turkey finds itself at the crossroads of globalization's paradoxes. The country holds an ambiguous identity, positioned between the West and its regional surroundings. On the one hand, Turkey ideologically and politically aligns with the West, actively participating in key institutions such as NATO and pursuing EU membership. However, it also diverges from the Western model due to geographical location, socio-political evolution, and economic structure. Furthermore, while Turkey is a predominantly Muslim country, it adheres to a secular system with an established democratic tradition. Beyond its NATO commitments, Ankara continues prioritizing a regional perspective in its security strategy.

---

[110] Coker, C. (2002). *Globalization and Insecurity in the Twenty-first Century: NATO and the Management of Risk*, Adelphi Paper 345, p. 52. London: IISS.

[111] Steinbrunner, J. D. (2002). *Principles of Global Security*, p. 146. Washington, DC: Brookings Institution.

Accordingly, the TAF implement military reforms to maintain operational effectiveness, whether cooperating with allies or independently.[112]

Turkey's security approach is shaped by two conflicting forces in the global system. Its EU candidacy, NATO membership, engagement in the Partnership for Peace (PfP), and participation in peacekeeping missions foster multilateralism, cooperative security, democratic oversight of the military, and a focus on societal and individual security. Conversely, its regional environment encourages reliance on power politics and the enduring centrality of the nation-state. Despite these competing dynamics, Turkey has demonstrated adaptability in aligning with global security transformations, particularly in relations with northern neighbors and peacekeeping initiatives. However, its security policies toward the Middle East and Greece have remained rooted in power-based frameworks, albeit primarily defensive. Recent developments—including the Iraq crisis, de-escalation in Cyprus, and improved Turkish-Greek relations—offer Ankara new opportunities to leverage globalization's benefits for enhancing security.

Global political trends are generally seen as more complex than economic or cultural trends, as they directly challenge the role of the nation-state in both domestic and international affairs. On the one hand, globalization weakens state authority in certain areas; on the other, it reinforces the state's relevance in managing the risks associated with interconnected security threats. This section examines Turkey's experience within this framework, posing two key questions: How has Turkey responded to major global security transformations? And what are the prospects for its successful adaptation? In addressing these issues, the analysis considers both the enabling and obstructing factors in Turkey's security adaptation process.

Security scholars broadly agree that globalization's impact on international security extends beyond the identification of new threats. Laurent Goetschel highlights three central dynamics that help us understand the evolving security landscape.[113] First, globalization has facilitated an expansion of political,

---

[112] Karaosmanoglu, A. L., and Kibaroglu, M. (2002). "Defense Reform in Turkey." In I. Gyarmati and T. Winkler (eds.). *Post-Cold War Defense Reform: Lessons Learned in Europe and the United States*. Washington, DC: Brassey's.

[113] Goetschel, L. (2000). "Globalization and Security: The Challenge of Collective Action in a Politically Fragmented World," *Global Society*, 14 (2), 276–277.

economic, and social interactions across inter-regional and intercontinental levels. Second, the increasing interaction between states and civil societies has heightened the importance of both "individual security" and "societal security," which involves the protection of cultural identities and values. This, in turn, has contributed to a growing sense of "global awareness" among individuals and communities. Third, globalization has led to a relative decline in the state's dominance in world politics, elevating the role of non-state actors, intergovernmental organizations, and non-governmental organizations (NGOs). A fourth critical dimension should also be noted: the diminishing relevance of traditional geopolitics.

Globalization has also contributed to the spread of universal norms, such as democratization, human rights, and the rule of law.[114] However, this process raises concerns about unilateral or arbitrary interventions in states that do not meet these standards, as was arguably the case in the second Gulf War against Iraq. In response, international law has increasingly adjusted to globalization's demands, particularly in revisiting the role of the United Nations in legitimizing military interventions. Traditionally, security studies have focused on the state as the primary actor, with "national security" narrowly defined in terms of territorial and regime security. However, globalization has prompted a significant shift in this approach.

International security has increasingly taken precedence over traditional national security, as the stability of individual states is now more closely tied to the security of the broader international system.[115] Growing interdependence reinforces the long-standing liberal argument that excessive threat perceptions and military buildups can create new instabilities, ultimately reducing security for all states. This suggests that national security cannot be approached in isolation—it must also consider the security of others. Additionally, contemporary threats, such as terrorism and the proliferation of weapons of mass destruction (WMDs), transcend national borders and

---

[114]   Finnemore, M. (1996). "Constructing Norms of Humanitarian Intervention." In Peter J. Katzenstein (ed.), *The Culture of National Security*, p. 182. New York: Columbia University Press.

[115]   Shaw, M. (September/October 2001). "The Development of the Common Risk Society," *Society* 7.

require international cooperation and risk management. This shift has given rise to the concept of "cooperative security."

Since the Cold War's conclusion, "cooperative security" has gained traction as a liberal alternative to balance-of-power strategies.[116] It emphasizes collaboration among states to mitigate, contain, or counteract security risks that could otherwise lead to conflict.[117] Unlike traditional collective security or collective defense, cooperative security incorporates two additional dimensions. First, it prioritizes "individual (or human) security," ensuring fundamental freedoms and protections for individuals. Second, it promotes and projects stability both within and beyond the cooperative security framework. This model assumes a direct connection between stability and the advancement of democratic values.[118]

The growing influence of non-state actors, including communities, political organizations, and ethnic groups, has increasingly challenged the traditional notion of national security. At the same time, NGOs play a more active role in security matters, often operating in strategically important regions alongside military forces. These non-state entities frequently have transnational connections while also serving as integral components of civil society. As a result, their security and protection are now recognized as critical considerations in modern security frameworks.[119] This shift reflects a broader transformation that began in international law in the nineteenth century.

One of the most significant consequences of globalization has been the changing role of geopolitics in security considerations. Traditional geopolitical thought viewed national security through a rigid, deterministic lens, treating geography as a fixed and immutable factor. National borders were regarded as unalterable parameters that dictated foreign and security

---

[116] Cohen, R. (April 2001). "Cooperative Security: From Individual Security to International Stability." In Cohen R. and Mihalka M. (eds), *Cooperative Security: New Horizons for International Order*, The Marshall Center Paper no. 3, p. 3.

[117] Ruggie, J. G. (1996). *Winning the Peace*, pp. 80–81. New York: Columbia University Press.

[118] Cohen, R. (April 2001). "Cooperative Security: From Individual Security to International Stability." In R. Cohen, and M. Mihalka (eds.), *Cooperative Security: New Horizons for International Order*, The Marshall Center Paper no. 3, pp. 5–10.

[119] Goetschel, L. (2000). "Globalization and Security: The Challenge of Collective Action in a Politically Fragmented World," *Global Society* 14 (2), 260.

policies.[120] However, in today's world, national security is no longer confined to fixed territorial boundaries but has expanded across multiple dimensions. A clear example of this shift is the challenge posed by transnational terrorism. Unlike conventional military threats, terrorism transcends state borders, creating a security environment in which the battleground is no longer strictly geographical but also extends into civilian and cyber spaces. Consequently, civil society plays an increasingly significant role in counterterrorism efforts. Lasting success in combating terrorism is unlikely unless states secure the trust and support of their populations.

Moreover, a country's geopolitical significance is no longer determined solely by its geographical location but also by various non-geographical factors. Elements such as democratic governance, foreign policy objectives, and strategic alignments now play a crucial role in shaping a state's influence on the global stage. In this regard, geopolitical power has become a matter of perception as much as physical positioning. As one American scholar aptly observes, "All national security strategies start with a mental image of the world." [121]

Despite these transformations, the state remains a cornerstone of security studies and policymaking. The principles of territorial integrity and national sovereignty continue to be fundamental concerns. However, the key distinction today is that globalization has introduced new security dimensions, which are now incorporated into traditional national security frameworks. Security is no longer exclusively a national issue—it has become an increasingly international and transnational matter.

Modern states now face risks beyond traditional military threats, such as cross-border conflicts. In many cases, ensuring state security requires active international and transnational cooperation, particularly in counterterrorism. The effectiveness of state protection is no longer measured solely by military strength but by its ability to engage in global security partnerships. Nevertheless, the state remains the most capable institution for ensuring the

---

[120] Tuathail, G. O. (1999). "Understanding Critical Geopolitics: Geopolitics and Risk Society." In C. S. Gray, and G. Sloan (eds), *Geopolitics: Geography and Strategy*, pp. 107–124. London: Frank Cass.

[121] Zelikow, P. (2003). "The Transformation of National Security: Five Redefinitions," *National Interest*, 71 (Spring), 17–28.

security of both individuals and civil society, as well as for managing risks associated with globalization. Additionally, the state plays a crucial role in regulating globalized markets, which form a key pillar of liberal and social democratic economic policies, particularly in Europe. Christopher Coker articulates this idea by emphasizing that globalization should be seen as a transformative process rather than a force that dismantles existing political structures. He argues that globalization does not eliminate territorial geography, territoriality, or supra-territoriality; instead, these elements continue to coexist and interact in complex ways. While globalization is undoubtedly reshaping social structures such as the state and the nation, it has not replaced them altogether.[122]

Ensuring human security in an era of global terrorism requires a proactive approach focusing on risk reduction. Effective counterterrorism efforts necessitate a combination of protective measures, the dismantling of terrorist networks, and the pre-emptive disruption of terrorist activities. However, these measures can only be carried out successfully through a strong state apparatus and inter-state cooperation. The state continues to hold the monopoly on organized armed forces and remains the only legitimate actor capable of enacting and enforcing national laws. Equally important in the fight against international terrorism is that international law itself is a product of state interactions. Legal norms are established through treaties and international agreements between states, making them central to shaping global security policies.[123]

Although globalization has somewhat reduced the exclusive role of states in international relations, they remain the primary actors in shaping security policies. Thus, the defining factor for determining a state's global standing is not whether its security policies are entirely state-centric but rather whether its security approach extends beyond national concerns. At the same time, political elites navigating globalization must recognize what has been described as "the relativization of the state"—a reality in which external forces and international obligations increasingly influence state sovereignty. The critical question is: How does Turkey address the

---

[122] Coker, C. (2002). *Globalization and Insecurity in the Twenty-first Century: NATO and the Management of Risk*, Adelphi Paper 345, p. 20. London: IISS.

[123] Stern, B. (2001). "How to Regulate Globalization." In M. Byers (ed.), *The Role of Law in International Politics*, pp. 250–251. Oxford: Oxford University Press.

security challenges brought about by globalization, and how far has it evolved beyond its conventional national security approach?

4.5. Turkey's Role in Cooperative Security

Following the end of the Cold War, Turkey increasingly prioritized regional cooperative security and peace support operations, expanding its engagement in a range of missions, from peacekeeping to peace enforcement. The country played a key role in peace support initiatives in Somalia, the Balkans, and Afghanistan, as well as in various peace observation missions. The Turkish Land Forces contributed at the brigade level to UNPROFOR in Bosnia, and in December 1995, their mission continued under SFOR. Meanwhile, the Turkish Navy joined "Operation Sharp Guard" in the Adriatic, enforcing an arms embargo on the former Yugoslavia. Similarly, in April 1993, the Turkish Air Force took part in NATO's "Operation Deny Flight," deploying an F-16 squadron from Italy's Ghedi air base to help enforce the no-fly zone over Bosnia and safeguard designated safe areas.

During the Kosovo crisis, Turkey further expanded its involvement by deploying a mechanized infantry battalion and headquarters personnel to KFOR, in addition to sending three Special Operations Teams to assist the Hostage Rescue Force. Moreover, Turkey contributed an F-16 squadron to NATO's "Operation Allied Force" in Kosovo. Beyond the Balkans, Turkey assumed leadership roles in the United Nations Operation in Somalia and played a key role in the International Security Assistance Force in Afghanistan. Although Turkey, as a non-EU NATO member, does not have full participation rights in the European Security and Defense Policy (ESDP) decision-making process, it has nevertheless signaled its readiness to contribute to the EU's "Headline Goal" by offering a brigade-level unit, supported by air force and naval resources.

Turkey's commitment to cooperative security extends beyond participating in peace support operations to include the establishment of regional security mechanisms. Ankara has played a leading role in forming the Southeastern Europe Multinational Peace Force (SEEBRIG) and the Black Sea Naval Cooperation Task Group (BLACKSEAFOR). Alongside joint harbor and maritime training designed to improve operational coordination, BLACKSEAFOR is structured to support search and rescue missions, humanitarian aid efforts, demining operations, environmental protection, and peacekeeping activities.

Peace support missions are often manpower-intensive and demand specialized skills and training. Given that the TAF primarily consists of conscripts serving only 18 months, those selected for peacekeeping roles receive specialized training tailored to combat readiness, public relations, and security enforcement in operational areas. Soldiers assigned to peace operations are often chosen based on foreign language proficiency, ensuring effective communication in multinational environments. To further institutionalize its role in peacekeeping, the TAF established new command structures, designating the 3rd Corps and the 28th Mechanized Brigade for peacekeeping missions. The Turkish General Staff and each military branch—land, navy, and air—also created dedicated Peacekeeping Departments.[124]

In the nineteenth century, multilateral military interventions were primarily driven by strategic interests and balance-of-power politics despite claims of humanitarian objectives. The Ottoman Empire frequently found itself targeted by European powers under such justifications. Similarly, during the Cold War, United Nations peacekeeping operations focused on preventing regional conflicts from escalating into direct superpower confrontations. In essence, peacekeeping at the time served to reinforce the stability of the bipolar international system. In contrast, modern peace operations have evolved into political and normative undertakings guided by universal values and democratic principles. Contemporary peacekeeping missions prioritize promoting democratic governance and countering authoritarian regimes that violate basic human rights and moral standards. This shift reflects a broader liberal approach to security, emphasizing that lasting peace and stability can only be achieved through adherence to shared international norms.[125]

Turkey has actively supported NATO's PfP program, engaging in regional military and naval exercises and establishing a PfP Training Center in Ankara.

---

[124] Karaosmanoğlu, A. L., and Kibaroğlu, M. (2002). "Defense Reform in Turkey." In I. Gyarmati, and T. Winkler (eds.), *Post-Cold War Defense Reform: Lessons Learned in Europe and the United States*, pp. 145–146. Washington, DC: Brassey's.

[125] Finnemore, M. (1996). "Constructing Norms of Humanitarian Intervention," In P. J. Katzenstein (ed.), *The Culture of National Security*, pp. 81–182. New York: Columbia University Press.

As part of its commitment to PfP objectives, Turkey has conducted training and educational programs in Azerbaijan and Georgia, extending its influence beyond its immediate borders. The PfP program serves a broader purpose than merely fostering military cooperation, interoperability, and transparency among NATO members and partner states. Much like NATO's enlargement strategy, its ultimate goal is to extend security and stability eastward by shifting away from balance-of-power strategies in favor of cooperative security frameworks. This transformation represents an effort to replace Cold War-era security approaches with a new paradigm based on collective security, democratic governance, and institutional cooperation. Through this lens, the PfP program is not only a military initiative but also a mechanism for orienting participant states toward the core values of the Atlantic Alliance and, indirectly, the European ideals represented by the EU.

Turkey's active engagement in NATO and its contributions to the PfP reinforce its Western identity and strengthen its standing within the Alliance. Its membership in Western security institutions, coupled with its strategic position bridging Europe and Eurasia, allows Turkey to project Western values to newly independent states in the Caucasus and Central Asia. However, Turkey faces significant challenges in fully capitalizing on this role. While it has made substantial democratic and liberal reforms in recent years, institutional shortcomings remain an obstacle to its long-term ambitions. Issues related to democratic governance, civil–military relations, and human rights have, at times, complicated its broader foreign policy objectives. Nevertheless, Turkey continues to pursue a dual-track strategy, maintaining its regional security commitments while aligning itself with Western security structures and norms.

4.6. Power Politics

During the Cold War, Turkey largely adhered to a policy of non-interference in Middle Eastern affairs, maintaining only limited engagement with the region. Alongside its European allies, Ankara opposed U.S. proposals to extend NATO's mandate to the Middle East and the Persian Gulf. Relations with Israel remained at a minimal diplomatic level, and Turkey's interactions with its Arab neighbors were mostly confined to trade. However, this cautious approach began to shift dramatically in the early 1990s. Turkey's foreign policy in the region became increasingly interventionist, unilateral, and grounded in power politics. This transformation was partly driven by Turkey's broader post-Cold War foreign policy activism. A key moment in this shift was President Özal's decision to join the international coalition against Iraq during the first Gulf War. This multilateral engagement continued with operations such as "Provide Comfort" and "Northern Watch." However, the most pressing factor behind Turkey's changing stance was the escalating threat of PKK terrorism and the absence of effective international cooperation in counterterrorism, which ultimately forced Ankara to take unilateral action.

Following the first Gulf War, the collapse of Iraq's central authority north of the 36th parallel introduced new security challenges for Turkey. This ungoverned space quickly became a safe haven for PKK militants, who used the region as a base to launch attacks on both civilian and military targets in Turkey. In response, the TAF conducted nearly seventy cross-border operations in northern Iraq between the two Gulf Wars, aiming to dismantle PKK camps and disrupt the group's logistical networks. The frequency of these incursions led to the establishment of a de facto security zone, with Turkish military forces maintaining a presence in the area to contain the PKK's activities.

Another key element of Turkey's strategy was applying military pressure on Syria. In the early 1980s, PKK leader Abdullah Öcalan and other high-ranking members of the organization took refuge in Damascus. The Syrian government not only provided them with safe haven but also offered financial and military support, including training camps in the Bekaa Valley. This backing significantly strengthened the PKK, enabling it to carry out cross-border attacks in Turkey. Despite Ankara's diplomatic efforts to persuade Syria to sever its ties with the group and expel Öcalan, Damascus repeatedly denied any involvement. The situation escalated until October 1998, when Turkey issued an ultimatum and deployed armored divisions to the Syrian border. The pressure worked—Syria ultimately agreed to expel Öcalan and cut its support for the PKK.[126]

---

[126] See Radu, M. (2001). "The Rise and Fall of the PKK," *Orbis* 45 (1) (Winter), 47–63.

The PKK, however, was not just a domestic threat—it was a transnational terrorist organization with deep connections across the Middle East and Europe. It received various forms of support from certain regional and European governments, as well as from NGOs. While the PKK's financial networks were largely based in Western Europe, Turkey found itself isolated in its counterterrorism efforts. Except for the United States, Ankara received little to no support from its neighbors or allies. Given the lack of meaningful international cooperation against the PKK, Turkey was left with no option but to take matters into its own hands.

Despite its unilateral efforts, Turkey's struggle against the PKK came at a high cost. While military operations significantly weakened the organization, the conflict resulted in approximately 30,000 casualties, left another 10,000 people wounded, and placed a severe financial burden on the country—costing Turkey an estimated five billion U.S. dollars per year. Even though Turkey managed to suppress PKK activities within its borders, the group remained active beyond them. An estimated 5000 armed PKK militants continued to operate in northern Iraq, attempting to position themselves as a third Kurdish force alongside the Kurdistan Democratic Party (KDP) and the Patriotic Union of Kurdistan (PUK). Ankara's primary concern was that any post-war instability in Iraq could create new opportunities for the PKK to reestablish itself and resume attacks on Turkish soil.

At the same time, Turkey embarked on a broad reform agenda aimed at liberalizing its political, legal, and economic systems. These reforms were primarily driven by the country's desire for further democratization and its ambition to meet the EU's membership criteria. Since August 2002, the Turkish Parliament has enacted a series of laws and constitutional amendments, representing a major step forward in Turkey's long-standing democratization efforts. One of the most significant legal changes was the abolition of capital punishment. Additionally, new legislation expanded cultural rights for ethnic minorities, particularly in broadcasting and education, allowing languages such as Kurdish to be taught and used more freely. Further reform measures sought to strengthen freedoms of expression and association while imposing stricter limitations on police powers. Meanwhile, the influence of the military over political decision-making was curbed through institutional reforms, including revisions to the composition and advisory role of the National Security Council. In parallel, the extraordinary security measures that had been in place in Turkey's southeastern regions for years were finally lifted. While challenges remain in the full implementation of these reforms, the process of aligning Turkey's legal and political systems with EU norms continues.

For Turkey, maintaining a peaceful regional environment and securing its borders is essential to sustaining this reform process. However, any fragmentation of Iraq or further instability in the region could threaten this progress. A power vacuum in Iraq could provide the PKK with the opportunity to reposition itself and resume its armed campaign against Turkey. If such a scenario were to unfold, Ankara might feel compelled to reintroduce harsh military measures and conduct cross-border operations into northern Iraq, further complicating regional stability and its diplomatic relations with the United States. Recent media reports suggest that Washington is aware of these risks and may take steps to disarm and dismantle the PKK's presence in northern Iraq, which could alleviate some of Turkey's security concerns.

Since its military defeat, the PKK has shifted its focus toward political activism, attempting to move its separatist agenda into the political sphere. The organization has already rebranded itself under the name KADEK and may intensify its political activities in both Turkey and Europe, particularly if U.S.-led counterterrorism efforts neutralize its remaining armed elements in Iraq. Turkey may face renewed instability if it fails to develop a long-term political strategy that prioritizes societal security—including social and economic policies alongside traditional security measures. Without a comprehensive approach, Turkey risks not only internal unrest but also increased international and transnational interference in its domestic affairs.[127]

Another key dimension of Turkey's evolving security policy in the Middle East has been its military cooperation with Israel. The two countries began to move closer in the late 1980s, culminating in the establishment of full diplomatic relations at the ambassadorial level in 1991. This paved the way for signing their first military cooperation agreement in April 1992. While Turkish-Israeli military collaboration does not constitute a formal alliance—since it lacks mutual defense commitments—it represents a highly advanced form of strategic partnership. This cooperation encompasses joint naval, air, and land

---

[127] Aydinli, E. (June 2002). "Between Security and Liberalization: Decoding Turkey's Struggle with the PKK," *Security Dialogue* 33 (2), 209–225.

exercises, shared training programs, mutual access to airspace, defense industry projects, and intelligence sharing. Due to the depth and intensity of this military partnership, many states in the Middle East perceive it as an informal alliance. Some analysts in both Israel and Turkey argue that this collaboration serves as a deterrent and strengthens coercive diplomacy. Indeed, there are claims that Turkey's military ties with Israel played a role in enhancing Ankara's credibility when pressuring Syria to expel Öcalan in 1998.[128]

In simple terms, Turkey jeopardized its own security to assist Western Europe during the Cold War, exposing itself to tensions and hostility from a neighboring superpower. This was done to help maintain the European military balance by controlling the Straits and engaging over 30 Soviet and Warsaw Pact divisions in the Black Sea region. In exchange, Ankara benefited from a clear defense commitment and deterrence, including backing from its European allies. It also received military and economic aid during peacetime, primarily from the United States and, to a lesser degree, from Germany. After the Cold War, this arrangement no longer met the strategic needs of the new era. The shift in the international system negatively affected Turkey's security ties with Europe. With the end of the Soviet threat, security commitments among allies weakened, and the focus of security challenges moved from the central front to NATO's southern region. Regional concerns came to the forefront, diminishing the impact of the global balance of power on regional politics, including the Middle East, which began to be treated on its own terms rather than in terms of the global system. By benefiting from this systemic flexibility, Turkey expanded its horizons and pursued a more active, assertive, and independent foreign and security policy, particularly in the Middle East. Turkey's newfound regional centrality ironically emphasized its differences from Europe, leading many Europeans to view Turkey as an added security burden. Issues such as Turkey's poor human rights record and the unresolved Kurdish question began to significantly shape European perceptions of Ankara in a negative light. Furthermore, rising prejudices against Islam after 9/11 and the emergence of various primordialist terrorist organizations, unjustly and wrongfully claiming that

---

[128] Inbar, E. (2003). *The Israeli-Turkish Strategic Partnership*, Ramat Gan: BESA, Bar-Ilan University.

they act in the name of Islam, created a divisive and nefarious impact on relations between Christians and Muslims.

Besides the changes in the international system, the last two decades have also drastically altered the domestic context of Turkey's foreign and security policy. These changes could be traced back to Turgut Özal, first Prime Minister, then President of the Republic from 1982 to 1993. The founding cadres of the Justice and Development Party (AK Party) were greatly inspired by Turgut Özal, who strongly attached to a free-market economy and modernization rather than an ephemeral, muddling-through approach to the economy and politics. He made the first attempts to combine Western patterns of economic growth and political and bureaucratic reforms on the one hand and Islamic values on the other. He also made successful efforts to change the state-controlled, protectionist economic structure. As a firm believer in liberalism, he opened up the country's economy to the world and introduced a perspective of economic interdependence into foreign relations. Moreover, he encouraged the emergence of a new conservative entrepreneurial middle class, motivating them to be competitive inside and outside. One of his significant achievements was perhaps his utmost care not to tilt the sensitive equilibrium between Western (and Westernization) and Islamic values, particularly in his rejection of strict Kemalist secularism (laicism).

Following Özal's footprints, the JDP (AK Party) has dramatically transformed Turkey since 2002. The Party's consecutive successes in general and municipal elections under the leadership of Recep Tayyip Erdoğan and Abdullah Gül provided it with the opportunity to change the polity and society. The EU reforms, including a moderate and liberal interpretation of secularism together with the freedom of religion and other fundamental rights and freedoms from 2002 to 2010, introduced a more democratic and pluralistic outlook in politics. The second great leap forward occurred through the AK Party's persistence in the security sector reforms. One of their most significant contributions to democratization in Turkey was putting an end to military encroachments upon politics; beyond this, they laid the groundwork for the military to voluntarily accept the democratic and strategic principle of "the primacy of politics." This has become particularly visible in military operations against the PKK and in the strenuous efforts to address the Kurdish question.

Another dimension of the transformation has resulted from the qualitative and quantitative growth of the provincial bourgeoisie and their becoming increasingly competitive inside and outside. Furthermore, the migration of conservative rural populations and small-town middle classes impacted the social and political life of the metropolises. Their interaction with people of a Western-oriented lifestyle, speaking the same common mother tongue, opened a convenient space for them to gradually adopt the codes and habits of urban life in the center. This social and political evolution, on the other hand, has rendered religion and conservatism more visible while providing the conditions to improve and strengthen Turkey's exceptional synthesis between Westernization and Islam. These developments also brought about political and social tensions, empowering suppressed identities—predominantly Islamic, Kurdish, and Alevi—and bringing them to the fore. The transnational character of these identities erased the borderline between international affairs and internal politics, adding complexity and ambiguity to policy-making. Thus, Ankara could not overlook external developments when dealing with domestic affairs and vice versa. The growing impossibility of isolating the international and the internal from one another led to a comprehensive and profound shift in Turkey's geopolitical priorities and strategic style. These changes confronted Turkey with difficult challenges but at the same time, increased the country's potential to elevate its status regionally and globally.

4.7. Turkey's Prospects in a Globalized World

In the final centuries of the Ottoman Empire, the ruling elite initiated a process of Westernization, aiming to formally integrate the state into the European state system as a core foreign policy objective. This trajectory accelerated with Atatürk's republican and secular reforms, which established Turkey as a nation-state, aligning it with the dominant state model in the West at the time. These reforms set Turkey on an irreversible path toward adopting Western norms and institutions. After World War II, democratization and the adoption of a multi-party political system became integral to Turkey's Westernization efforts. While embracing liberal economic policies remained partial, Turkey's commitment to multilateralism and cooperative security initiatives—particularly in the Black Sea region and the Balkans—helped temper its power politics approach following the Cold War.

Turkey's NATO membership since 1952 and its involvement in the Alliance's integrated defense planning and command structure have strengthened a sense of internationalism within the Turkish military. Turkey is already highly globalized in various sectors, including business, the defense industry, tourism, telecommunications, digital connectivity, higher education, and academic research. The country is a member of the ECU and has recognized the compulsory jurisdiction of the European Court of Human Rights (ECHR), signaling its commitment to the broader European legal and economic framework.

Despite these advancements, globalization challenges the traditional nation-state model by introducing a range of social, cultural, political, and economic transformations that interconnect nations worldwide. This shift has diminished the capacity of any single state to exert complete control over its own trajectory, effectively leading to a curtailment of state sovereignty. In response, traditional state elites often perceive globalization as a threat rather than an opportunity, preferring inward-looking policies emphasizing national autonomy over international engagement. This inclination frequently results in the securitization of domestic and economic issues, making legal, political, and economic reforms more difficult to implement.

Two central aspects of globalization directly impact national security: the relativization of the state's importance and the diminishing role of traditional geopolitics. While the state remains essential in managing the risks of globalization, the increasing influence of non-state actors, civil society, and international organizations has somewhat reduced its dominance. Turkey has voluntarily accepted certain limitations on its sovereignty through international treaties, institutional memberships, and legal commitments, such as its participation in the ECU, human rights conventions, and the jurisdiction of the ECHR—not to mention its economic agreements with the IMF.

However, from a contemporary international legal perspective, these commitments are not considered infringements on sovereignty. Instead, they reflect an exercise of sovereign will, demonstrating Turkey's strategic choice to engage with the global order. Furthermore, these obligations are not irreversible—a government, assuming political responsibility for the consequences, could theoretically withdraw from such agreements. However, such a retreat would be another exercise of sovereignty, albeit one that could come with serious economic and geopolitical costs.

Turkey's security relationship with the EU offers a case study of how glo-balization has shaped its geopolitical significance. For many years, Turkey's strategic approach rested on the assumption that its geopolitical importance made it indispensable to European security, believing this would encourage the EU to adopt a more flexible stance on Copenhagen political criteria and a more favorable position regarding the Cyprus dispute. However, this perspective overlooked a key factor: Turkey's geopolitical relevance is shaped by the EU's own perception of geopolitics rather than by Turkey's self-assessment.

Firstly, the EU views itself as a "security community" focused on tran-scending traditional power politics and classic geopolitical concerns. Its primary objective is to foster peace and stability by promoting democratic ideals, which are core to its identity. From this standpoint, Turkey's ability to enhance its geopolitical standing concerning the EU depends less on its strategic location and more on the strength of its democratic institutions. Second, the EU has only recently started considering a more active role in global politics. While many European policymakers acknowledge Turkey's objective geopolitical importance, they do not necessarily view it as indis-pensable to achieving Europe's long-term security objectives.

Turkey's success in cooperative security initiatives in the Black Sea region and the Balkans is largely attributed to its membership in NATO and strong integration into the Western security community. Equally important was the regional states' willingness to engage with the West, which facilitated Turkey's security partnerships.

However, the Iraq crisis highlighted the relative nature of Turkey's geo-political significance. Ankara's mismanagement of the crisis, particularly regarding its refusal to allow U.S. forces to use Turkish territory for a northern invasion of Iraq, led to a diminished perception of its strategic value—at least from an American perspective. At the same time, however, many European governments and the public viewed the Turkish Parliament's decision as a democratic act, strengthening Turkey's democratic credentials in the eyes of Western audiences.

Moving forward, Turkey's geopolitical relevance will depend not only on its strategic location but also on its ability to consolidate its democracy, enhance its democratic identity, and project shared Western values to Eurasia and the Middle East, particularly in countries such as Iraq.

Turkey has reached a critical juncture. The time has come to reassess traditional geopolitical assumptions in light of new global realities. While this transition may be challenging and even unsettling, resisting globalization would come at a higher cost than embracing it. As a partially globalized nation, Turkey would risk significant setbacks should it attempt to retreat from international integration. Such a withdrawal would disrupt Turkey's economic, political, and security relationships with key international actors, jeopardize its economic growth, and diminish its influence in regional and global affairs. Furthermore, increased alienation from the West could push Turkey toward a more unilateralist and power-driven foreign policy, potentially straining its relationships with European and transatlantic allies.

The future of Turkey-EU relations is particularly important in this context. EU policies will unquestionably shape Turkey's domestic and international trajectory.[129] A clear and credible membership perspective could urge Ankara to pursue greater security cooperation in regions such as the Eastern Mediterranean and the Middle East. Conversely, continued alienation from the EU could exacerbate tensions with Greece, heighten regional security concerns, and push Turkey toward unilateralist policies grounded in traditional power politics. Ultimately, Turkey's ability to navigate globalization will depend on its willingness to embrace democratic reforms, strengthen its institutional framework, and engage constructively with its Western partners. The cost of stagnation is high—but the cost of further globalization presents greater opportunities for economic growth, security partnerships, and geopolitical influence.

4.8. Principles of Turkish Foreign Policy

Prime Minister Ahmet Davutoğlu identifies several guiding principles of Turkish foreign policy applicable in the current political and strategic context. He emphasizes that "Turkey's foreign policy is shaped by a comprehensive understanding of historical trends and a sense of proactive involvement... The country's position is influenced by its historical background, geographic location, and extensive legacy in global relations." He also underlines the

---

[129] See Stephen Larrabee, F., and Lesser, I. O. (2003). *Turkish Foreign Policy in an Age of Uncertainty*, pp. 195–199. Santa Monica, CA: RAND.

necessity of careful consideration of his country's own conditions and to "make revisions where necessary." This emphasis on prudence is pertinent. The point, however, is whether revisions and adaptations are made in time, without delay.

Since foreign and security policy-making is an ongoing exercise that requires adaptation to current conditions, we cannot avoid the future as well as the past. The present and future political and strategic contexts must be evaluated and extrapolated from past developments. However, we must be very careful in seeking causal connections from the past to the future, as such connections are rare. Another important point to remember is that history is not always clearly and correctly understood; it is open to various interpretations and, therefore, may be uncertain and misleading. Similarly, the future will never offer us objective facts. Thus, no matter how creative, policy-makers will still need to refer to history. This need becomes particularly heavy in times of transformation. This depressing situation, however, can be remedied to some extent by "good" historians, who could warn policy-makers against prejudiced interpretations, simplistic analogies, and conspiracy theories. Neither historians nor policy-makers are able to predict the future, but the former can at least prevent the latter from misusing the past.

Turkey shares a common history with the Balkans and the Middle East. Ankara believes that this common history has the potential to reconnect the peoples in these regions. The historical and cultural propinquity might offer the parties concerned a common destiny. This objective constitutes one of Turkey's policy priorities and should not be sacrificed to material political and economic interests. Prime Minister Davutoğlu emphasizes that this aim will continue to guide Turkish foreign policy: "We will not take steps that will alienate us from the hearts and minds of our region's people."

At this point, it is useful to say a few words on neo-Ottomanism, which is often referred to in defining and criticizing Turkey's current foreign policy. The so-called neo-Ottoman tendencies of the JDP governments imply a certain desire to come to terms with Turkey's Ottoman and Muslim heritage, which the Party believes was overlooked by previous governments. Critics of the AK Party's policies assert that this is a very strong reference that suggests imperialism, hegemony, and domination. It is true that, in the government's discourse, the reference to the Ottoman past occasionally carries a strong emphasis. However, it is not more than a historical call for the above-mentioned cultural closeness to the regional peoples of the neighborhood. It is far from an irredentist or imperial ambition. This could be seen as a factor motivating Turkey's pursuit of greater international prominence, aiming to secure a stronger and more favorable position in surrounding regions. It also suggests that Turkey has a multicultural legacy. It is hoped that recognizing past multiculturalism could serve as a legitimizing soft power discourse in dealing with the Kurdish question and in playing a mediatory role in various regional conflicts.

Another important aspect of neo-Ottomanism is its aspiration to synthesize Western values and Islam. Following the example of Özal, the AK Party leadership is undoubtedly aware of this duality in the Ottoman history of modernization. This complex amalgamation has had a social and political reformist impact on the Republic. The high momentum of Westernization in the Republic, together with a radical secularization and the adoption of Western norms and institutions, paved the way for Turkey's membership in Western international organizations such as NATO and the Council of Europe after the Second World War. However, this development was far from sufficient to overcome the centuries-old dualism of the Ottoman past. On the contrary, within the "new" foreign policy framework, this dualism is regarded as a valuable asset to increase Turkey's freedom of action in foreign affairs. This way of thinking, however, is not peculiar to the AK Party governments; it was also visible in previous administrations.

Nevertheless, a great number of critics argue that the present administration has tipped the balance toward the Islamic and Middle Eastern characteristics of Turkey. Turkey's Ottoman past has a double-edged sword effect in the Balkans and the Middle East. While it facilitates friendships with certain states and communities, it may complicate relations with others due to the existence of religious and sectarian conflicts. In political and social contexts, emphasizing the Ottoman past may be more of a burden than an asset.

Finally, despite numerous successful democratic reforms, Turkey still has serious human rights problems. Its democracy requires consolidation. Deficiencies in its democratic regime tend to decrease the credibility of its role as an example and promoter of the democratic and liberal values of the West. Nevertheless, in recent years, the government has been working hard to balance freedoms and security at home. This has become an important principle in the fight against terrorism, motivated by the conviction that stability and peace cannot be developed based on force alone. The continuation of democratic politics is required for the legitimacy of using force, as well as for the successful implementation of a security strategy against the terrorist organization PKK.

Turkey pursues a value-oriented foreign policy, embracing Western and Muslim values and promoting shared values. The President of the Republic and the Prime Minister often emphasize these values. Values considered the common heritage of humanity, such as justice, equality, democracy, and support for those suffering from severe deprivation and cruelty, are frequently highlighted by these leaders. This highly humanitarian discourse distinguishes the current political leadership not only from previous Turkish leaders but also from most leaders worldwide. Moreover, they do not refrain from strongly criticizing those who violate these values, including allies.

On the other hand, however, the foreign and security policy pays utmost attention to the defense of political independence and territorial integrity. Maintaining autonomous decision-making and policy formulation has always been an important priority for Turkish leadership, particularly in the post-Cold War era. As has been the case so far, Ankara continues to coordinate its policies with its Western allies, as it does not see them as harmful to Turkey's vital or major national interests.

Turkish foreign and security policy is vision-oriented and has a long-term perspective. Long-term economic and defense policies are usually formulated as consecutive periodic plans. "Vision-oriented" foreign policies and their implementation require both daring and caution. The ability to adapt, timely shifts from unilateralism to multilateralism, patience, and convenient wiggle spaces are necessary to successfully manage the strategic outcomes of a "vision-oriented" foreign policy.

Security cooperation with allies, or at least policy coordination, has become a complex and challenging. First, public opinion pressure has increasingly weighed on decision-makers in Turkey, as well as in the United States and among European allies. It has become very difficult to decide and act within the framework of national interests. Public opinions can now impose their own values, convictions, perceptions, and sensitivities on political authorities. For instance, Turkey could restore friendly relations with Israel much more easily during the Cold War than today. In taking steps toward rapprochement, the government would find itself awkward, inevitably considering the risk of losing votes. A similar position would be relevant for the Allies as well.

Under the burden of growing Islamophobia, they may not wish to appear as yielding to the demands of an Islamic government.

Contrary to the old one, Turkey's new foreign policy is not made and pursued in a world of reliable guarantees and manageable ambiguities; instead, it must be formulated in a dynamic environment with diversified actors and implemented through high-risk operations. The recent decades have drastically altered the global and regional configuration of power within which Turkish foreign and security policy operates. Since the early 1990s, it has been studied in three consecutive stages. Although each stage radically differed from the standard assumptions of the previous decades, they also displayed varying characteristics among themselves. In recent decades, Ankara has exhibited activist (and proactive) strategic behavior in its neighboring regions. Its activist behavior toward the allies, especially the United States, has evolved from pluralism, bilateralism, and cooperation to unilateralism, assertiveness, and a growing degree of autonomy.

During the first stage, from 1990 to 1995, Turkey became active, vociferous, and, to some extent, interventionist. Its policies, however, remained within the framework of allied interests. It strove to align its values and policies with its Western allies. Turkey promoted regional institution-building activities and participated in peace operations, especially in the Black Sea basin and the Balkans. For instance, Turkey's involvement in the Balkan War of the 1990s largely followed American actions. Ankara promptly recognized the independent statehood of Slovenia, Croatia, and Bosnia-Herzegovina and viewed the war against these nations as flagrant Serbian aggression. Ankara urged its allies to mobilize against Serbia, assertively underlining its own policy. At the same time, Ankara actively participated in the allied arms embargo in the Adriatic. It also participated in peacekeeping operations and other military operations together with allies. During that period, Turkey and the United States showed that they were able to accommodate their respective interests and consider each other's sensitivities. American attitudes toward Turkey's new activism can be defined as "selective encouragement," which gradually shifted to tolerance and "forbearance."

The second stage is characterized by two contradictory tendencies. On the one hand, circumstances urged Turkey, its allies, and Russia to strive to accommodate their interests on certain security and economic issues. On the other hand, a number of political irritants divided Turkey's interests from those of the United States and European allies. The third stage began as a result of Russia's military intervention in Syria and the downing of a Russian jet by Turkey's F-16s. The deterioration of the conflicts in Syria, escalating to a conventional war, will have various strategic consequences. First, Russian air operations will not only strengthen Assad's Baath regime but also secure Moscow's political and military presence in the Middle East and the Eastern Mediterranean. Putin's objective is also to create a favorable demographic environment for himself and Assad by forcing considerable portions of the Syrian population into neighboring countries, particularly Turkey (an ethnic cleansing strategy). Third, Putin has another strategic expectation that could have broader consequences beyond the Middle East. Bombings of Syrian towns and cities, such as Aleppo, will drive large numbers of refugees to Europe via Turkey. This would drive among EU and NATO allies, turning them into irresolute rivals to Moscow and weaker allies for Washington.

Recent events have brought Turkish foreign and security policy to a turning point. Ankara now needs to renew its confidence in NATO and the West, implying a revival of Turkey's Western vocation. Turkey should not give the impression that its policies and implementation are oriented toward a confrontational vision with the West. Instead, it should strive to present a clear perspective on its own fundamental values and vital (and major) security interests, which may differ but are not incompatible with those of its Western allies. Turkey's unilateralism should be moderated with a certain degree of reasonableness. Strategic challenges emanating from the North and the South cannot be met concerning national means only. Functional alliance relationships and effective international cooperation will be essential to a successful, vision-oriented activist policy. It should be acknowledged, however, that any multilateralism, particularly within alliance politics, will impose its own limitations.

Historical and Philosophical Considerations

5.1. The Hermeneutic Tradition and Its Influence on Turkey's Secularism Debate

We turn to Andrew Davison's *Secularism and Revivalism in Turkey: A Hermeneutic Reconsideration*. Before delving into his work, it is useful to begin with an introductory note on hermeneutics, its definition, and its objectives. Hans-Georg Gadamer (1900–2002), one of the most influential hermeneutic philosophers, integrated insights from linguistics and interpretative studies into his philosophical framework. In contrast to the organized and systematic methodologies of the natural sciences, he emphasized the interpretative and philosophical nature of human understanding.

At its core, hermeneutics is the art of interpretation and understanding. Gadamer argued that understanding is an ontological process rather than an epistemological one—meaning it is about being rather than merely knowing. He strongly opposed methodological dogmatism, criticizing the scientific mind's universal validity claims and asserting that historical consciousness and social context are unavoidable in human interpretation. While he rejected objectification, he did not embrace absolute relativism, maintaining that a degree of universal consensus in interpretation is possible. [130]

Following Martin Heidegger's influence, hermeneutic philosophy branched into two major traditions. The first, the hermeneutic tradition, developed

---

[130] Davison, A. (1998). *Secularism and Revivalism in Turkey: A Hermeneutic Reconsideration*, pp. 134–188. New Haven and London: Yale University Press; Cevizci, A. (2010). *Felsefe Sözlüğü*, pp. 690–692, 770–771. Istanbul: Paradigma; and Skirbekk, G., and Gilje, N.

around Gadamer and was rooted in the works of Schleiermacher and Dilthey. The second, the deconstructionist tradition, evolved through thinkers such as Jacques Derrida, Michel Foucault, and Richard Rorty. The hermeneutic tradition builds upon Heidegger's early work, focusing on understanding and interpretation as fundamental aspects of human action. While Heidegger initially concentrated on human behavior, Gadamer shifted the focus to historical texts, viewing them as key to developing a hermeneutical philosophy. In contrast, deconstructionists sought to "get behind the text," identifying contradictions and tensions that authors may have overlooked. [131]

This distinction between hermeneutics and deconstructionism highlights two contrasting intellectual orientations: one that respects tradition as a source of meaning (Gadamer) and another that seeks to radically critique and destabilize tradition (Derrida, Foucault). Despite their differences, both traditions were critical of modernity—Gadamer lamented the cultural decline of modern society, while deconstructionists viewed modern rationality as an implicit system of discipline and control.

To fully appreciate Davison's arguments, it is important to briefly outline Gadamer's philosophy. Heidegger's interpretation of philosophical texts profoundly influenced Gadamer, who introduced Heidegger's thought in his 20s. In his seminal work, Wahrheit und Methode (Truth and Method, 1960), he developed a philosophy of interpretation that sought to elucidate the conditions necessary for human understanding to occur. Unlike earlier hermeneuticists such as Schleiermacher and Dilthey, who focused on understanding texts within their historical context, Gadamer argued that interpretation is a dialogue between the text and the reader. His concept of the "hermeneutic circle" extends beyond the text to include the author's intellectual journey, cultural influences, and lived experience. However, Gadamer was skeptical of reducing interpretation to a psychological or historical project. Instead, he emphasized that a text inherently makes truth claims that must be evaluated on their own terms.

(1999). *Felsefe Tarihi*. Translated by Emrullah Akbaş and Şule Mutlu, pp. 578–582. Istanbul: Kitapevi.

[131] Skirbekk, G., and Gilje, N. (1999). *Antik Yunan'dan Modern Döneme Felsefe Tarihi*. Translated by Emrullah Akbaş and Şule Mutlu. Istanbul: Üniversite Kitapevi.

For Gadamer, understanding a text is not about immersing oneself in an author's intellectual life but about engaging with the meaning of the text itself. He posited that the truth claims of a text must be taken seriously before they can be properly interpreted—an approach known as Vorgriff der Vollkommenheit (anticipation of perfection). Two fundamental linguistic-philosophical points arise from this:

1. Language is central to human understanding—not just as a tool for communication but as a horizon of meaning that shapes our worldview. It is neither an objective set of symbols nor merely a national, linguistic structure; instead, it is an inherited framework through which we make sense of reality.

2. The meaning of a text is not a fixed object—it emerges only in relation to the interpreter's own horizon of meaning. This means that interpretation is always shaped by the historical and cultural perspective of the reader. [132]

When a text and its interpreter share the same historical and cultural background, the process of interpretation is relatively straightforward. However, when the text belongs to a different historical or cultural context, the challenge becomes greater. This is where Gadamer's concept of the "fusion of horizons" (*Horizontverschmelzung*) comes into play: understanding occurs when the interpreter's horizon and the text's horizon are brought into dialogue without necessarily merging into a single perspective. Thus, interpretation is not about arriving at an ultimate truth but about broadening one's own frame of reference—a lifelong process of intellectual formation (*Bildung*). Gadamer insists we can never fully step outside history to achieve a purely objective interpretation. Instead, we are always engaged in a dynamic process of learning and transformation. [133]

---

[132]　Skirbekk, G., and Gilje, N. (1999). *Antik Yunan'dan Modern Döneme Felsefe Tarihi*. Translated by Emrullah Akbaş and Şule Mutlu. Istanbul: Üniversite Kitapevi.

[133]　Skirbekk, G., and Gilje, N. (1999). *Antik Yunan'dan Modern Döneme Felsefe Tarihi*. Translated by Emrullah Akbaş and Şule Mutlu. Istanbul: Üniversite Kitapevi.

Davison extends hermeneutic inquiry to studying secularism and modernity in Turkey, drawing upon Dankwart Rustow[134], Binnaz Toprak[135], and Ziya Gökalp to illustrate the complex relationship between Islam, nationalism, and modernization. He argues that Turkey's secular model (laiklik) has been mischaracterized—rather than a strict separation of religion and state, it has historically functioned as a system of state control over religion.[136] As an intellectual, Ziya Gökalp actively engaged with the profound transformations of his time, articulating them conceptually in two interrelated ways. First, he redefined the key concepts of "nation" (millet), "religion" (ümmet), and "modernization" (muasırlaşma), giving them new meanings that reflected the evolving social and political landscape. Second, he provided a fresh interpretation of the relationship between Turkish national culture, Islam, and modern civilization, addressing the challenges posed by rapid political, economic, social, and ideological change. Gökalp argued that the crucial distinction between culture and civilization was central to understanding how Turks could maintain both their national cultural identity and Islamic religious heritage while selectively integrating aspects of modernity.

To fully understand this aspect of Gökalp's thought, it is essential to consider his background in Sufi Islam and his education within an Islamic intellectual tradition. He was not only a historian of Islam but also widely recognized as a mentor (mürşid) in this context. His conviction that a modern state should distinguish between religion and politics in order to engage with international civilization while maintaining cultural integrity distinguishes him from the laicist policies of Kemalism. While Gökalp saw secularization as a means of protecting cultural and religious authenticity, Kemalist secularism (laiklik) sought to institutionalize state control over religion, effectively

---

[134] Rustow, D. (1957). "Politics and Islam in Turkey 1920-1955." In R. Frye (ed.), *Islam and the West*, p. 70. Hague, Mouton & Co.

[135] Toprak, B. (1988). "The State, Politics and Religion in Turkey." In M. Heper, and A. O. Evin (eds.), *State, Democracy and the Military: Turkey in the 1980s*, p. 120. Berlin and New York: de Gruyter.

[136] Davison, A. (1998). *Secularism and Revivalism in Turkey: A Hermeneutic Reconsideration*, New Haven and London: Yale University Press, pp. 134–188; Atay, F. R. (1969). *Laicism in Çankaya, 1981–1938*, pp. 444–448. Istanbul: Doğan Kardeş Yayınevi (English edition in this book).

subordinating religious institutions to the authority of the state in an effort to impose a particular vision of modernization.

The Kemalist approach took the separation of religion and state seriously enough to implement legal and administrative reforms that aimed to remove religious influence from public affairs and reshape religious practice within a state-controlled structure. However, Gökalp's vision of Islam as an ethical system within an evolving Turkish culture suggests that, had the Kemalists followed a similar perspective, they might have opted for a more nuanced secularization process—one that established control but without excessively centralizing religious oversight. Instead, the reforms pursued under Atatürk's leadership did not merely limit the role of religion in politics. Still, they institutionalized a system of state oversight over Islam, ensuring that religious institutions remained under strict governmental supervision.

Thus, rather than achieving a clear separation between religion and the state, Kemalist reforms ultimately resulted in partial separation within a framework that reinforced state control over society. In certain dimensions, this even expanded state influence over religious institutions. While there was an effort to remove religious authority from governance, the mechanisms of religious reestablishment under state control were never fully dismantled. Disestablishment remained incomplete, and the secular state retained direct oversight over religious institutions and practices, ensuring that Islam remained a regulated element of national identity rather than an independent force within society.

Davison argues that hermeneutic inquiry cannot be confined to either a narrowly secular or religious perspective. Instead, it must remain critical and open-ended, challenging both conservative and positivist interpretations of history. He also calls for a deeper hermeneutic study of secular politics in Turkey, recognizing that tradition and modernity are not opposing forces but interconnected dimensions of political life. While Davison's work represents an important contribution to political thought in Turkey, it remains incomplete in addressing the broader implications of Mustafa Kemal Atatürk's political and military legacy. Understanding Atatürk's role requires comparative historical analysis, as well as a strong foundation in military and legal history—areas that Davison's study only touches upon.

The discussion of Turkey's legal reforms brings us to the adoption of the Swiss Civil Code, which was chosen for its modern and systematic structure.

While the Mecelle, the Ottoman legal code, was seen as a step forward in its time, it was ultimately deemed incompatible with contemporary civilization and Turkish national life.[137] However, legal modernization in Switzerland was itself a gradual process shaped by federalism and historical traditions. Classical jurisprudence practices—such as the designation of husbands as family leaders—remained in effect in some Swiss cantons until the 1970s.[138]This demonstrates that secularization and legal reform are complex, evolving processes rather than sudden transformations.

Turkey stands at a pivotal moment, requiring a reconsideration of its historical, political, and legal trajectory. As globalization reshapes national sovereignty, Turkey must balance its unique cultural identity with its engagement in international legal and political systems. Understanding this dynamic requires a hermeneutic approach, one that acknowledges historical context, linguistic meaning, and the evolving nature of political authority.

5.2. Charles Taylor and Hermeneutics

Taylor begins his well-known work, *Philosophy and the Human Sciences (Interpretation and the Sciences of Man)*, with a question: "Is there a sense in which interpretation is essential to explanation in the sciences of man?" There is an inevitably "hermeneutical" component in the sciences of man, as seen in the interpretations of Freud and Habermas and the beginning of the writings of Gadamer. Taylor argues that hermeneutic interpretation involves clarifying or making sense of a given object of study. This object is typically a text or something resembling a text that appears confusing, fragmented, contradictory, or otherwise unclear. The purpose of interpretation is to uncover an underlying sense or coherence within it. Consequently, any field that qualifies as hermeneutic, even broadly, must engage with complex and intertwined forms of meaning. According to Taylor, this process requires two essential components. First, there must be an object or set of objects that can be evaluated in terms of coherence or the lack thereof—essentially,

---

[137] Davison, A. (1998). *Secularism and Revivalism in Turkey: A Hermeneutic Reconsideration*, pp. 197–203. New Haven and London: Yale University Press.

[138] Dürrenmatt, P. (1958). *Histoire de la Suisse: la Confédération et l'État Fédératif* La Fondation de l'Etat Fédératif, Payot, pp. 87–166.

something that can be understood as making sense. Second, there needs to be a discernible distinction, however subtle, between the meaning itself and the medium through which it is conveyed, such as words or symbols. Without this separation, the task of clarifying what is disjointed or confusing would become impossible.

Taylor argues that a successful interpretation reveals the initially obscure, fragmented, or unclear meaning. The question arises: how can we be certain that an interpretation is accurate? According to Taylor, the validity of an interpretation lies in its ability to make sense of the original material. When aspects that once seemed puzzling, contradictory, or difficult to grasp become comprehensible, it suggests that the interpretation is on the right track. This process relies on our grasp of the language, enabling us to recognize the initial confusion or contradictions. The interpretation, by presenting the meaning in a clearer, more coherent form, resolves these uncertainties.[139]

For Taylor, the goal of hermeneutical inquiry is to replace an individual's incomplete or mistaken self-interpretation with a more accurate one. To achieve this, scholars must examine the self-interpretation and the behavioral context in which it occurs. He draws an analogy to interpreting historical documents, where understanding the surrounding events is crucial. However, this analogy is imperfect, as hermeneutical analysis requires interpreting both the interpretation and the behavior simultaneously.

This process raises the question of whether the meaning uncovered through interpretation can fully align with the original. Taylor suggests that this issue is particularly relevant in the field of politics. Political behavior consists of actions that might appear as objective data, but these actions are deeply connected to the actors' subjective meanings. The pursuit of objective political science has often focused on isolating quantifiable aspects of behavior, which is in line with empiricist principles. Yet, Taylor contends that this approach risks neglecting the interpretive, meaning-based nature of human actions, which remains central to the hermeneutical sciences.[140]

---

[139] Taylor, C. (1985). *Philosophy and the Human Sciences*, p. 15. Cambridge: Cambridge University Press.
[140] Taylor, C. (1985). *Philosophy and the Human Sciences*, p. 55. Cambridge: Cambridge University Press.

Taylor concludes *Philosophy and the Human Sciences* by emphasizing that human sciences inherently look to the past, as they are fundamentally historical. He argues that these sciences are grounded in universally accepted intuitions and are deeply connected to our core moral and ethical positions. In this sense, the human sciences are moral sciences in a more profound way than eighteenth-century thinkers recognized. Taylor notes that this idea is not novel—Aristotle articulated a similar perspective in *Book One of the Ethics*. However, Taylor suggests that this notion remains unsettling and difficult to reconcile with the dominant frameworks of modern scientific thought.[141]

As far as Charles Taylor inspires me, I believe his most significant philosophical and historical turning point is explained in Chapter 16, "The Providential Order," in his great book *Sources of the Self: the Making of Modern Identity*.[142] Until then, most people viewed eighteenth-century Deism as a staging area on the way to political secularism and the unbelieving Enlightenment. We could probably argue that Deism only prepared the way for the radical Enlightenment. There was only one important way to get over these paradoxes: what would lead one to praise and be thankful to God if one saw his work useful, successful, and meaning kindness and understanding to other people? This goodness is called "benevolence," and at the beginning of the Scottish and Irish Enlightenment, Francis Hutcheson (1694–1746) used this word as a philosophical term. Charles Taylor is interested in Hutcheson's work; however, he defines "benevolence" as the mutual positioning and implementation of secularism and Deism together. Hutcheson argues that a deep sense of love and gratitude toward God is essential. He believes the soul's highest and most expansive inclination toward universal happiness can only be centered on the original, independent, and omnipotent Goodness. Without understanding this Goodness and having a passionate love and submission to it, the soul cannot achieve its "most stable and highest perfection and excellence."[143] The key point here is the focus on humanity. It is human

---

[141] Taylor, C. (1985). *Philosophy and the Human Sciences*, p. 57. Cambridge: Cambridge University Press.

[142] Taylor, C. (1989). *Sources of the Self: The Making of the Modern Identity*. Cambridge, MA: Harvard University Press.

[143] Taylor, C. (1989). *Sources of the Self: The Making of the Modern Identity*, pp. 248–265. Cambridge, MA: Harvard University Press.

happiness that holds true significance in the universe. Ethical, emotional, and modern human identification lies in that benevolent combination.

In his research works, Charles Taylor was never completely satisfied or dissatisfied. Within this paradoxical endgame of Taylor, the goal was to replace his disorganized, incomplete, and somewhat inaccurate self-interpretation. Much like interpreting a historical document requires situating it within the flow of related events, understanding self-interpretation involves placing it within the broader context of behavioral patterns. For instance, the usual and standard norms were acceptable behaviors that made sense. Taylor suggests that moral reality relies on the presence of human beings, as moral reasoning emerges from their efforts to understand their moral experiences—particularly the concept of "benevolence." Consequently, the considerable majority of the radical Enlightenment peoples rejected the constitutive good of Deism and the providential order. However, at the same time, they wanted to try their notion of dignity and central significance in their outlook. Taylor, however, was in favor of "the ideal of universal and imperial benevolence." Taylor argues that the Deist view of providential order emphasized the significance of human life and its everyday fulfillment. Pursuing these fulfillments for oneself and ensuring them for others gained greater importance, as they were seen as part of a divinely endorsed plan.[144]

Taylor suggests that before examining political science, it is worth considering whether the sciences of human behavior are inherently hermeneutical. He questions what leads us to view humans and their actions as objects that fit the criteria for hermeneutic analysis. The continuing interpretations of historical documents could improve the condition of a hermeneutical science. Thus, in scientific study, it is not the legitimacy of a political movement itself that is considered, but rather the perceptions or sentiments of the individuals who are members of that movement regarding its legitimacy.

Taylor's *Sources of the Self* explores how modern conceptions of personhood have evolved, highlighting both the positive aspects and the potential limitations of this understanding. It examines the influential role of the Protestant Reformation (and also the Catholic Church, which was not merely oppositional) in shaping this development, as well as the contributions of the

---

[144] Taylor, C. (1989). *Sources of the Self: The Making of the Modern Identity*, pp. 266–284. Cambridge, MA: Harvard University Press.

Enlightenment, which enhanced self-awareness and the notion of self-mastery. As Taylor suggests, a religion driven by fear, where individuals are motivated by the expectation of reward and punishment, suppresses true piety, which involves loving God for His own sake. In moral theory, he suggests that pain and pleasure serve as the criteria for right action, not based on how they affect the individual but on their impact on everyone. Bentham wanted to foster a "culture of benevolence" in society, potentially extending its lifetime and historical power. The theories of radical Enlightenment and its materialist utilitarianism are challenging to clarify because they contain two conflicting elements: a reductive ontology and a moral power that are difficult to reconcile. Despite these difficulties, however, *Sources of the Self*, at the end of the huge book, was still trying to find a fundamental expression without complicating radical Enlightenment humanism and modern moral predicament.

Charles Taylor particularly emphasizes the significance of Jean-Jacques Rousseau and the Romantic movement. Romantic love and integrated emotions exceed power and intention.[145] He examines the long-standing debate over instrumentalism in detail, as it has been central to discussions of modernity for the past two centuries. His goal is to shed light on modern identity by interpreting this debate within its broader context. He hopes this approach offers some new insights. Ultimately, he presents a perspective that critiques many prevailing interpretations for being too limited, arguing that they fail to fully acknowledge the diversity of values and, consequently, the conflicts and dilemmas that arise from them.[146] Taylor suggests that while some may argue that wisdom requires judiciously stifling our spiritual aspirations, assuming that they inevitably lead to destruction or mutilation, he rejects this as our unavoidable fate. He views the dilemma of spiritual mutilation as a significant challenge rather than a predestined outcome. Though he acknowledges the difficulty of fully demonstrating this, Taylor points to the hope inherent in Judaeo-Christian theism despite its historical failings, particularly in the promise of divine affirmation of humanity. He notes that elaborating on this would require an entire book. Still, he clarifies that his

---

[145] Taylor, C. (1989). *Sources of the Self: The Making of the Modern Identity*, p. 518. Cambridge, MA: Harvard University Press.
[146] Ibid., pp. 513–514.

goal in this conclusion is to show how his understanding of modern identity can help us better understand the moral issues of our time.[147]

As I have already pointed out, Taylor never accepted ignoring radical political decisions and their military implementations by central governmental organizations. The Philosopher in modernity was profoundly aware that the theoretical and historical context could disappear. Taylor's monumental *A Secular Age* is arguably the most influential work ever published on the phenomena of security, spanning a wide range of disciplines, from the poetic and social sciences to deeply philosophical realms. It has profoundly impacted discussions in sociology, history, anthropology, and religious politics.

As I said before, Taylor questioned the idea that secularization directly results from the scientific and rational progress of the radical Enlightenment. Thus, because of this correct understanding, Taylor employed his language (words, terms, adj., nouns, etc.) very softly. For example, in his use of the word "induction," which usually means introducing someone into a new job, company, official position, or industrial work (a state got ready to wage war or fighting), he means to persuade or influence someone to do some things (to convince a state or a group to act against a mutual enemy). To "industrialize" can mean establishing or developing a military-industrial complex for oneself or one's allies. Charles Taylor's philosophy is guided by strong ethical commitments and public concerns, which are, at the same time, ordered by the central and regional governments.

We know that Taylor places special emphasis on Jean-Jac Rousseau and the Romantics. These can build up their accounts of the human self by integrating elements such as romantic love, emotions, and aesthetics and by embracing nature in newly positive ways. Moreover, it was emphasized that language played a vital role in this expression, alongside art, religion, actions, and ethical relationships. Human expression varies across different cultures and even among individuals. This diversity did not stem from a rigid human nature but was enabled by humanity's innate capacities. Therefore, bridging what could be seen as the Enlightenment and Romantic aspects of the modern self requires both the quest for self-understanding and self-control, as well as unique self-expression and authenticity.

---

[147] Ibid., p. 521. You can also see "Charles Taylor Has Reimagined Identity and Morality for a Secular Age," London: *LSE* (London School of Economics), 2016.

Taylor has played a crucial role in shaping our understanding of the "politics of identity," which, he argued, stems from a fundamental human need for recognition. Individuals do not simply possess identity in isolation; instead, it develops within social contexts where people seek validation from others. As Taylor noted in 1994, this need for recognition extends to identities that can be politically mobilized, such as nationality, race, ethnicity, gender, or sexuality. He emphasized that "due recognition is not just a courtesy we owe people. It is a vital human need." Treating individuals with dignity and respect requires acknowledging their diverse social contexts, particularly those whose identities have been historically marginalized or denied equal treatment. Taylor's broader concerns center on how language shapes human identity—how it exists only through shared use and serves not just as a tool for communication but as an essential element of human existence.

As far as I know, Taylor did not write about Mustafa Kemal Atatürk, his thoughts, or his politics. However, despite this lack of togetherness, Mustafa Kemal's ideology and its application interestingly resembled Charles Taylor's ideas, especially regarding the influence of language, modernity, and secularism on human beings, as well as the ideal of universal and impartial "benevolence"—but without prohibiting the use of military power when necessary. We have already studied in detail how Mustafa Kemal familiarized himself with the political, philosophical, and military knowledge of van der Goltz Pasha and Clausewitz. Shortly, this was related to the process of cognition: knowing, understanding, learning, and realizing.

After Atatürk's death, Turkey's major conservative political parties of the 1960s limited themselves to their rightist or leftist descriptive perspectives and simplistic analysis. This fundamental turn encouraged the Armed Forces to integrate with political decisions and actions. So, the military took over or, at least, intervened in and controlled civilian institutions. When the Islam-inspired and, at the same time, modernizing Justice and Development Party (JDP) came to power, two of the founding members of AKP, Abdullah Gül, who was the President of the Republic of Turkey (2007–2014), set up an intellectual advisory group. The President and Prime Minister Recep Tayyip Erdoğan accepted the final report of this institution. Since then, the Turkish Armed Forces have absolutely civilized and democratized their relationships with other people and institutions. Moreover, in a very short period, they have advanced in areas like economy, technology, operational art, strategy, etc. Officers who rejected military reforms were expelled from the armed forces and other state institutions.

5.3. Lebow's Theory of International Relations

In classical Greek Philosophy, especially by Plato and Aristotle, it was suggested that the psyche is composed of three distinct drives—appetite, spirit, and reason—each pursuing its own objectives. In modernity, the focus shifted toward valuing ordinary life, emphasizing material well-being over the classical ideals of virtue and salvation. The spirit was de-emphasized due to its links with the aristocracy, while appetite gained prominence, being reframed as a driver of economic growth and political stability. Meanwhile, reason was reduced to a purely instrumental function. As Plato and Aristotle recognized, this transformation led to a widespread need for what is now referred to as "self-esteem." The spirit seeks autonomy through material means because it is essential to the goal of self-assertion. Conventional paradigms of politics and diplomacy are uprooted by this desire. Ned Lebow notes that liberalism describes politics as material interests, while realism acknowledges their primacy after security.[148] He believes that culture and ideas are a camouflage for political, economic, and military realities. Just as individuals strive for ontological security, states also seek a stable sense of self, which they develop and maintain through established foreign policy practices.[149]

Ontological security suggests that identities are built upon diverse narratives and values, which, once established, create strong incentives for leaders to act in alignment with them or justify their decisions accordingly. A key aspect of identity is self-esteem, which is sustained through the pursuit of honor and status. Examining this dynamic—both at the individual and state level—offers valuable insight into often-overlooked motivations behind state behavior. The prevailing view sees actors as independent, self-interested, and largely ahistorical, assuming that political analysis should focus on their decisions. In contrast, rationalist theories argue that these decisions are

---

[148] Lebow, R. N. (2008). *A Cultural Theory of International Relations*, p. 15. Cambridge: Cambridge University Press.

[149] Lebow, R. N. (2008). *A Cultural Theory of International Relations*, pp. 22–26. Cambridge: Cambridge University Press.

shaped, if not entirely determined, by external pressures and constraints. Constructivists then start working. Military strategic theories cannot be framed and limited by the IR theory.[150] Strategy is not a static construction; it is a developing process. It should change according to historical currents and how actors interpret them. Not all social scientists operate within the positivist framework; many focus instead on exploring the underlying conditions and cultural contexts that shape social and historical reality, giving meaning to both actors and their actions. While some social scientists adopt positivist methodologies, others are more interested in understanding cultural resources and the historical and intellectual conditions that shape social-political reality and make agencies (actors and their actions) meaningful: "The *Verstehen* and *Erklärung* traditions resort to theory, albeit to different kinds (causal explanations)."[151]

5.4. Stigmatization and History

The concepts of stigma and stigmatization have recently been included in the discipline of International Relations. Stigma has no unifying character; on the contrary, it has a separating character. Stigmatization marks the targeted people as disgraceful. I would argue that stigmatization is a useless term for a better understanding of the history of international relations, as it dismisses accurate and rightful studies.

In his interesting article on "Stigma Dynamics and the Crisis of Liberal Ordering," Adrian Rogstad of the University of Groningen made two contributions:

> Primarily, to the literature on stigma in international relations, it has added a distinction between diffuse and direct stigmatization and a broader focus on stigma dynamics—the relational unfolding of stigmatization processes depending on the various approaches taken by both the stigmatized and the 'audience of normals.' Secondly, to work on the crises of liberal order, it has provided an example of the kind of relational contestation of liberal ordering that is becoming

---

[150] Lebow, R. N. (2008). *A Cultural Theory of International Relations*, p. 53. Cambridge: Cambridge University Press.
[151] Lebow, R. N. (2008). *A Cultural Theory of International Relations*, p. 34. Cambridge: Cambridge University Press.

more acknowledged in the literature, explored through the case of Russian stigma management vis-a-vis liberal norms since the 1990s.[152]

The article has offered several integrated concepts, such as liberal ordering, stigmatization, identity management, and the "normal" state in international society. The article concludes with a question: This suggests that the future of liberal ordering is not predetermined or linear. Viewing liberal order as a process implies that crises in liberalism are always relative, often gradual, and can potentially be reversed. These changes are part of the ongoing dynamics of relative ordering and disordering, as well as the interplay of stigmatization and counter-stigmatization. Instead of a singular, dominant "normal" emerging, it is more likely that various "normals" will coexist in tension, with the processes of stigmatization failing to firmly impose one over the others.

This perspective suggests that the future of liberal ordering is not fixed but rather a continuous, evolving process. The crisis within the liberal order is viewed as relative and gradual, with the potential for change or reversal depending on ongoing processes of both organization and disorganization. Rather than a single dominant "normal" taking shape, it is more probable that multiple "normals" will exist simultaneously, causing tension, with the processes of stigmatization unable to solidify one over the others. Andrian Rogstad notes, "While Zarakol is right that stigmatization can hold the world together, it can also make it fall apart when actors seek to manage their stigmas in more confrontational ways."[153]

While preparing my book, I will not be in a position to deal fundamentally with all the details in the interesting publication by Ayşe Zarakol, titled *After Defeat: How the East Learned to Live with the West*. In 1648, the leading European states decided to establish the Westphalian system among the Christian Europeans. However, the system was far from being successful during its first centuries. The Napoleonic Wars and the two World Wars were the most destructive and unlawful wars in Europe. I would prefer not to extend the discussion of Zarakol's well-known book for two simple and

---

[152] Rogstad, A. (2022). "Stigma Dynamics and the Crisis of Liberal Ordering," *Global Studies Quarterly*, 1–11.

[153] Rogstad, A. (2022). "Stigma Dynamics and the Crisis of Liberal Ordering," *Global Studies Quarterly*, 1–11.

fundamental reasons: she did not attempt to soften (or somewhat modify) her basic arguments.

> Turkey, Japan, and Russia all pre-date the Westphalian system as political entities. As empires, they long sustained social universes capable of producing comprehensive worldviews. In other words, before their incorporation into the Westphalian system, these states had their own normative standards by which they defined themselves as "normal" and others as different, abnormal, or inferior.[154]

The Westphalian system reached its peak in the nineteenth century. This change did not have any influence (good or bad) on the three states (Turkey, Russia, and Japan), as Zarakol explained in her theories. Whereas Turkey and Russia had learned how to live with Western Europe, at least from the sixteenth century onward, through integrated formulations of autonomous institutions and organizations. There were many other integrated formulations in economics, science, technology, arts, and armed forces. Unfortunately, many modern IR theorists have dismissed the works of great historians. Such disregard could certainly prompt a reconsideration of these questioned theories.

The radical Enlightenment rejected the concept of providence or a divine plan. Its ethical framework was grounded entirely in utility, starting with the belief that individuals seek happiness or pleasure and aim to avoid pain. The central concern is how to maximize happiness. From this viewpoint, decisions about right and wrong cannot be based on any understanding of the order of things, either the ancient hierarchy.

It has frequently been pointed out that the psychological underpinnings of utilitarianism are somewhat inconsistent with its ethical principles under the governance of pain and pleasure. In its moral framework, pain and pleasure serve as the standards for determining the right actions, not based on their effect on individuals but on their impact on everyone. The goal is to achieve the greatest happiness for the greatest number. Theories of materialist utilitarian Enlightenment are hard to bring into focus. They have two sides: a reductive ontology and a moral impetus, which are difficult to combine,

---

[154] Zarakol, A. (2011). *After Defeat: How the East Learned to Live with the West*, p. 9. Cambridge: Cambridge University Press.

as inductive ontology does not easily align with epistemological morality. In any case, such an ontology cannot produce or sustain moral power.

Taylor's influential works on secularism—spanning poetic, social scientific, and philosophical dimensions—have significantly shaped debates across disciplines such as sociology, history, ontology, epistemology, and state religious policies. The prevailing ontology views actors as independent, self-centered, and often without a historical context, focusing on responsibility and control. In contrast, rationalist theories suggest that these choices are influenced, if not entirely determined, by environmental factors and constraints. This is where constructivists begin their work. However, strategy theory cannot be developed solely based on IR theory.

Ayşe Zarakol explains the diplomatic relations of Russia, Turkey, and Japan with the Western great powers. She said:

> Turkey is a country that has bent itself out of shape for almost a century to join the Western world while at the same time holding on to the worst kind of paranoid suspicions about Western intentions... The exaggerated sense of pride and the persecution complex exhibited by Turkish nationalism today is not an inherent tendency of Turks, but rather the unfortunate consequence of Turkey's place in the international system. However responsible Turks may be for their conduct, the underlying causes of such behavior can be found only in the interactions between Turkey and international society throughout the last century.[155]

This means that Turkey carries a stigma. Ayşe Zarakol, referring to Erving Goffman, describes "stigma" as a special discrepancy between virtual and actual social identity.[156] A stigmatized person is discredited or at least discreditable. Modern Turks constantly fear the possibility of being discredited; if their stigma is not apparent or immediately recognizable, they are still vulnerable to being discredited. They worry about being forever stuck with their stigma: Eastern, Asian, backward, Muslim, uncivilized, barbaric, etc.[157]

---

[155] Zarakol, A. (2011). *After Defeat: How the East Learned to Live with the West*, pp. 1–2. Cambridge: Cambridge University Press.

[156] Zarakol, A. (2011). *After Defeat, Cambridge Studies in International Relations*, p. 3. Cambridge: Cambridge University Press.

[157] Zarakol, A. (2011). *After Defeat, Cambridge Studies in International Relations*, pp. 3–4. Cambridge: Cambridge University Press.

Stigma, therefore, involves internalizing a specific normative standard that renders one's attributes discreditable; it serves as a label of difference and a moral principle imposed externally. This reflects the growing influence of modernity, driven by two key aspects: the belief that the scientific method can be applied universally and the rise of nationalism and "scientific racism."[158]

The social impact of the considerable rise took place in the West during Enlightenment: especially through industrialization and technological advancement. The European society of states and its standard of civilization must be in need of Enlightenment. The globalization of the outsider dynamic is a distinctive feature of the modern international system. In other words, the issue of relative strength was no longer viewed merely as a disparity in material capabilities; it had transformed into a moral, social, and cultural matter, embodying an existential dilemma at its core.[159] Some reformist groups, and even some conservative leaders such as Sultans like Mehmet the Conqueror and Suleiman the Magnificent, and many others contributed to reforms and established commercial and military relations with European powers. This mutuality has continued from the mid-fifteenth century to the second millennium. Moreover, identity management strategies between Turkey and Western Europe persist through social mobility, competition, and creativity. However, sometimes, states integrate various strategies into their foreign policies.

Christian Delacampagne argues that American philosophy has encouraged ethics and politics in the twentieth century, influencing fields such as music, theater, jurisprudence, and religion. Since 1917, this has become one of the most important philosophical and political turning points. However, if the nation-state is neglected, I believe an increasing number of philosophers will most probably remain insensitive to these developments. Despite this potential insensitivity, Delacampagne mentioned Tocqueville, Charles Alexis, and the establishment of a democratic federation in the United States.[160]

---

[158] Zarakol, A. (2011). *After Defeat, Cambridge Studies in International Relations*, p. 50. Cambridge: Cambridge University Press.

[159] Zarakol, A. (2011). *After Defeat, Cambridge Studies in International Relations*, pp. 53–56. Cambridge: Cambridge University Press.

[160] Delacampagne, C. (2010). *20. Yüzyıl Felsefe Tarihi*, Çev. Devrim Çetinkasap. Türkiye İş Bankası Kültür Yayınları.

Ayşe Zarakol did not want to limit herself to great philosophers such as Hegel, Kant, Nietzsche, and others. This is why the changes that Hegel celebrated as the progress of reason were criticized by other observers of modernity—from Burkes to Tönnies, from Tocqueville to Nietzsche:[161] "Tocqueville, who among the authors mentioned above was the most observant and also the most tolerant of what was lost in the transition to the modern age of democracy, was very much aware of this fact..."[162]

---

[161] Tocqueville, *Democracy in America* (Vol. II, 3, Chapter 19).
[162] Zarakol, A. (2011). *After Defeat, Cambridge Studies in International Relations*, pp.71–77. Cambridge: Cambridge University Press.

Conclusion

6.1. The School of the Enlightenment and Counter-Enlightenment

Azar Gat asserted that the notion that war could be systematically studied through historical analysis by selecting effective forms of organization and replicating successful strategies originated in ancient times. This approach saw a strong resurgence during the Renaissance, with a focus on practical application. It paralleled the classical tradition of political philosophy, the deductive understanding of history, and the concept of a universal natural law. Military theory at that time was essentially a blend of the best military practices from cultural history, particularly from Greece and Rome. According to Gat, from antiquity to Machiavelli's era, the technological aspects of warfare, and consequently its nature, had changed very little. Despite some variety in military models, these weapon systems remained largely unchanged, revealing recurring fundamental traits over time.[163]

Machiavelli's focus on military matters is clear: he saw the use of force as crucial in both domestic and international politics. Consequently, military topics appeared throughout his political works, culminating in his specialized treatise, *The Art of War* (1521). In this work, he aimed to extract the key lessons of military history and apply them to the design of an army suitable for his time. For Machiavelli, the militia—a national army of citizens

---

[163] Gat A. (1989). *The Origins of Military Thought from the Enlightenment to Clausewitz*, p. 1. Oxford University Press.

defending their homeland—was the ideal form of military organization, both socially and militarily.[164]

Machiavelli believed that the militia, a national army made up of citizens defending their homeland, was the ideal form of military organization from both social and military perspectives. This view was supported by history, particularly in the flourishing periods of the Greek city-states and the Roman Republic. In more recent times, it explained the remarkable strength of the small Swiss Republic. Conversely, history also showed the dangers of relying on mercenary armies, as seen in the decline of Greece and Rome. In the modern era, this was further confirmed by the disloyal, greedy, treacherous, and cowardly condottiere, who were more of a threat to their employers than to their enemies and contributed to the downfall of Italy's once-powerful city-states. During his career in the Florentine Republic's Chancellery and as Secretary of the Office of Ten, Machiavelli witnessed the harmful effects of Florence's reliance on condottieri and played a key role in efforts to rebuild the Florentine militia.

Machiavelli argued that infantry, equipped with close-combat weapons, protected by armor, and organized in dense formations, could generally withstand even the fiercest cavalry charges. This principle has been proven many times by the Greeks and Romans. For this reason, Machiavelli believed that infantry should form the core of a well-structured army.[165] Like his political writings, Machiavelli selectively used historical examples to support his arguments. His focus was primarily on theory rather than on history itself. However, his military ideas soon faced the impact of a significant historical shift. While Machiavelli was writing and publishing *The Art of War*, traditional methods of warfare were being transformed, largely due to the advent of firearms.[166]

The new arquebuses and firearms could not be integrated into the traditional military framework. Attempts to downplay their importance or to

---

[164] Gat A. (1989). *The Origins of Military Thought from the Enlightenment to Clausewitz*, p. 2. Oxford University Press.

[165] Gat A. (1989). *The Origins of Military Thought from the Enlightenment to Clausewitz*, pp. 2–3. Oxford University Press.

[166] Gat A. (1989). *The Origins of Military Thought from the Enlightenment to Clausewitz*, p. 4. Oxford University Press.

incorporate them as a "new type" of archers or slingers quickly failed. As stated by Gat, some have tried to explain away or minimize Machiavelli's disregard for firearms, even as they were becoming increasingly crucial in the Italian wars of the late fifteenth and early sixteenth centuries. Felix Gilbert, for instance, noted that in *The Discourses* (II, 17), Machiavelli's stance on artillery was intentionally biased to emphasize the importance of bravery. While Machiavelli's focus on moral strength is undisputed, his views on firearms cannot be seen merely as rhetorical. This is particularly clear in *The Art of War*, which Gilbert doesn't address in this context. *The Art of War* presents Machiavelli's comprehensive plan for army building and fully expresses his military philosophy. His ideal army is modeled entirely on Roman and Macedonian-Swiss structures, and although artillery is mentioned, its role in battle is significantly downplayed.[167]

Although now known only to a small group of scholars, Raimondo Montecuccoli (1609–1680) was considered in the eighteenth century, much like Clausewitz has been in the past two centuries—an outstanding modern military thinker whose highly regarded and influential writings laid the groundwork for a general theory of war. Born in 1609 to a noble family near Modena in northern Italy, Montecuccoli joined the Imperial Army and served actively throughout the 30 years' war, where he rose to the rank of general and earned distinction as a cavalry commander. After the war, he undertook diplomatic missions and led the Imperial forces in the Nordic war in Poland. His most significant victory came in 1664 when he defeated the Turkish army at the Battle of St. Gotthard. In 1673, during Louis XIV's Dutch War, he led his most famous campaign against Turenne on the Rhine, a campaign admired throughout the eighteenth century as a model of military maneuver.[168]

Montecuccoli is one of the most significant military figures of the seventeenth century. Still, he is also a strategist with solid foundations, an intellectual thinker, and a skilled historian with profound and extensive observations. He studied a wide range of philosophies, from the works of

---

[167] Gat A. (1989). *The Origins of Military Thought from the Enlightenment to Clausewitz*, pp. 5–6. Oxford University Press.

[168] Gat A. (1989). *The Origins of Military Thought from the Enlightenment to Clausewitz*, p. 13. Oxford University Press.

ancient Greek philosophers to Roman law and the Enlightenment writings of the Renaissance. He interpreted all these works in his mind to design the ideal and orderly army of a powerful authority.[169]

In his renowned work *On the War against the Turks in Hungary*, written late in life, Montecuccoli provided a sophisticated explanation of this process, drawing directly from Aristotle's *Metaphysics* (A.I.) and closely following its analysis. He emphasized the close relationship and mutual dependence between theory and practice: while theory is rooted in reality, it also serves to guide and evaluate actions. Each is vital to the other. In Montecuccoli's work, much like a mathematician, the first part presents the principles of the art of war, while the second part applies them—like deductions—to the battle against the Turks in Hungary.[170] He cites Lorini, a prominent Italian expert on fortifications from the late sixteenth century, who asserted that fortifications were a science governed by rules and mathematical principles, much like medicine. Reflecting the seventeenth-century *esprit géométrique*, the study of military geometry became a popular activity at European courts. In *On the War*, Montecuccoli followed an intellectual and educational framework established by various military writers from the latter half of the sixteenth century. He emphasized that decimal arithmetic, spatial calculations, and trigonometry were essential skills for the art of war, dedicating the first three chapters of his work to teaching these subjects systematically.

Montecuccoli's writings, likely considered state secrets and circulated only within select circles, were not published during his lifetime. However, when *On the War against the Turks in Hungary* (also known as *Aphorisms*) and *On the Art of War* were released in the early eighteenth century, they gained widespread readership. The works were translated into all major European languages (except English) and, within roughly a hundred years, saw multiple editions: seven in Italian, two in Latin, two in Spanish, six in French, one in Russian, and three in German.[171] With historical examples and a questioning

---

[169] Doğan. N. (2018). *Osmanlı-Habsburg Savaşlarında bir General: Raimondo Montecuccoli ve Tercüme-i Fenn-i Harb (1660-1664)*. Hacettepe University, History Department, M.A. Thesis, p. 153.

[170] Gat A. (1989) *The Origins of Military Thought from the Enlightenment to Clausewitz*, pp. 21–22. Oxford University Press.

[171] Gat A. (1989). *The Origins of Military Thought from the Enlightenment to Clausewitz*, pp. 22–23. Oxford University Press.

mindset shaped by the novel perspectives of Enlightenment ideas, he outlined the reforms he deemed necessary in the military field and demonstrated how an army organized in this manner could surpass the Ottoman army. This is because Raimondo Montecuccoli was keen on identifying the weaknesses of the Ottoman Empire, which he analyzed across a broad spectrum. Montecuccoli transformed the fear of the Turks, which was still widespread and dominant in his era in Europe, from a taboo into an analyzable subject. By developing his observations through scientific methods, he devised numerous tactics and strategies to counter this fear.[172]

It is certainly no coincidence that Montecuccoli frequently addressed issues such as the numerical superiority of the Ottoman army, their artillery and ammunition, the Janissary corps, and the timar system in his works. This is because he greatly admired the Ottoman military structure of his time. His admiration drove him to frequently observe Ottoman units in the Hungarian region. Through a comparative method, he identified the shortcomings of the Austrian army in comparison to the Ottomans, emphasizing the need for reforms. Regarding strategy, he notes a proverb before the details: "If a soldier is smart and intelligent, he does not need anything else." Because, in his opinion, the most glorious victory should not be won by fighting in the fields but by defeating the enemy with the power of the mind.[173]

As a result of his victory at the Battle of Saint Gotthard, Montecuccoli was appointed head of the Viennese Court War Council (Hofkriegsrat) in 1668. Now intent on concretizing the theories he had experienced, observed, and developed throughout his life, Montecuccoli established an academy called Écoles Militaires (Military Academy). He explained that this academy not only covered theoretical lessons, weapon usage techniques, and practical applications but also had an approach that ultimately focused on practice. It is particularly significant that Montecuccoli stated that in the war academy he established, he took the Janissaries of the Ottoman Empire as a role model

---

[172] Doğan, N. (2018). Osmanli-Habsburg Savaşlarında bir General: Raimondo Montecuccoli ve Tercüme-i Fenn-i Harb (1660–1664). Hacettepe University, History Department, M.A. Thesis, pp. 153–154.

[173] Doğan, N. (2018). Osmanli-Habsburg Savaşlarında bir General: Raimondo Montecuccoli ve Tercüme-i Fenn-i Harb (1660-1664). Hacettepe University, History Department, M.A. Thesis, pp. 90–91.

and recorded that individuals were recruited and trained under a system parallel to the *devşirme* system to ensure complete obedience. This statement demonstrates that the seventeenth-century Ottoman military system was closely studied and emulated within the Habsburg Court, one of the major empires of Europe at the time. It also reveals the extent of admiration a foreign military strategist—Montecuccoli, the pioneer of the military revolution in the seventeenth century—had for the structure and principles of the Ottoman army.[174]

However, the military thinkers of the Enlightenment showed little interest in Montecuccoli's specific military ideas. By the eighteenth century, with advancements in military strategy, his concepts had become outdated, and this was somewhat unsettling to Enlightenment thinkers, who favored universal principles. However, Montecuccoli's theoretical vision and conceptual framework were admired and widely adopted. Enlightenment thinkers were, fortunately, unaware of the precise nature of Montecuccoli's scientific pursuits, which likely would have shocked them. Instead, they resonated with his general intellectual assumptions. It wasn't the particular kind of science he practiced that mattered, but his scientific mindset. Montecuccoli formulated a sophisticated new theoretical approach to studying war, reflecting an emerging worldview. While the impact of firearms was acknowledged to some extent, it was overshadowed by the belief in universal rules and principles—an outlook inspired by science and driven by the growing intellectual effort to apply reason to all areas of life.[175]

Most Enlightenment thinkers were not particularly interested in physics, nor did they explore the mathematical complexities of science. For them, Newtonian science symbolized the power of the human mind to comprehend and control reality, and they aimed to apply its impressive achievements across the entire intellectual realm. They viewed the scientific model as a universal method for grounding all human knowledge and activity in critical empiricism and reason. This shared ideal transcended the many differences

---

[174] Doğan, N. (2018). Osmanli-Habsburg Savaşlarında bir General: Raimondo Montecuccoli ve Tercüme-i Fenn-i Harb (1660-1664). Hacettepe University, History Department, M.A. Thesis, pp. 104–105.
[175] Gat A. (1989). *The Origins of Military Thought from the Enlightenment to Clausewitz*, pp. 22–23. Oxford University Press.

among the *philosophes*, who were divided on issues such as deism versus atheism, dualism versus materialism, natural law versus utility, progress versus primitivism, and political systems such as enlightened absolutism, aristocracy, and democracy. Despite these notable differences, the common belief in this scientific approach fostered a strong sense of unity across all cultural domains. This cohesion extended to a broad, educated community whose social elite gathered in salons, embraced the idea of universal knowledge, believed that humanity could understand everything, and eagerly supported any new effort to uncover the universal principles of each discipline. All aspects of human culture and natural phenomena were to be brought under intellectual control, and war was no exception.[176]

Enlightenment military thinkers believed that the art of war could be systematically structured, relying on universal rules and principles drawn from the campaigns of history's great military leaders. However, war could not be entirely formalized, as these rules and principles always needed to be adapted to specific situations by the strategic brilliance of the general.[177] As Gat argues, a deep feeling of inferiority in military organization and doctrine led to a willingness to pursue extensive reforms and experiments, which made the French army the most progressive in Europe. These efforts shaped many of the military tools later used by the armies of the Revolution and Napoleon. Meanwhile, the Prussian army emerged from the Seven Years' War as the finest in Europe, with Frederick the Great's generalship universally admired. While Frederick's genius was seen as a quality that couldn't be easily analyzed, attention focused on the organization and doctrines of the Prussian army. Prussian success was believed to come from perfecting the firepower and maneuverability of linear formations operating in close order. As a result, there was a widespread belief that the French army needed a battle formation that could rival and even surpass the Prussian model. In the 1760s and especially the 1770s, French military thinkers concentrated entirely on developing such a formation. However, they all agreed on one point: the French should not try to match the almost mechanical perfection of Prussian

---

[176] Gat A. (1989). *The Origins of Military Thought from the Enlightenment to Clausewitz*, pp. 27–28. Oxford University Press.

[177] Gat A. (1989). *The Origins of Military Thought from the Enlightenment to Clausewitz*, p. 29. Oxford University Press.

drill and battle order. From Folard to du Picq, Foch, and Grandmaison, French military theorists held that the French people were too impulsive and imaginative to be subjected to the rigid discipline of the "phlegmatic" Prussians or to match their endurance. Instead, French enthusiasm, initiative, aggressiveness, and combative spirit allowed for more flexible and adaptable military doctrines.[178]

The organization of armies and their combat doctrines falls under the domain of "tactics." As Gat asserts, the meaning of this concept in the eighteenth century has often been misunderstood by later readers. Although it originated with the Greeks, the term was rarely used before the eighteenth century. Enlightenment military thinkers used "tactics" in its original Greek sense, referring to the system of army organization and battle formations. However, by the 1760s and especially the 1770s, as they focused on this area, viewing it as central to military theory, they expanded the term to encompass the art of war as a whole. Additionally, because they saw battlefield conduct as primarily a result of formation and related doctrines, "tactics" also came to mean the conduct of battle itself. It was only at the century's end, with Bülow, that the concept evolved to its modern meaning: the art of conducting battle. Moreover, Maizeroy's writings revolve around the search for the ideal system of tactics. In the debate between column and line formations, he took a moderate stance, favoring the *ordre profond*.[179]

The conduct of operations formed the second crucial aspect of the art of war. Maizeroy coined the term "strategy" for this branch, although its roots in modern military theory appear to have been overlooked. Maizeroy, who translated Byzantine military texts into French, played a pivotal role in introducing the term derived from the Greek word for general, which was used by Emperor Maurice in his military treatise *Strategicon*. Maizeroy first employed the term "strategy" in 1777 in his later work, *Théorie de la guerre*. The concept was slow to gain traction in the French military language and was still almost unknown in Britain at the start of the nineteenth century. However, in Germany, where Maizeroy's work was widely read, and a German

---

[178] Gat A. (1989). *The Origins of Military Thought from the Enlightenment to Clausewitz*, p. 38. Oxford University Press.

[179] Gat A. (1989). *The Origins of Military Thought from the Enlightenment to Clausewitz*, p. 41. Oxford University Press.

translation of Leo's was published in 1781, the term quickly became accepted and was already part of military literature by the 1780s. Bülow later divided the conduct of operations into "strategy" and "tactics" as they are understood today. This usage spread across Europe in the nineteenth century through his works and German military literature.[180]

A thorough scientific examination of the politico-military realm must analyze all these factors in detail. Guibert notes that he has not yet accomplished this in the *Essai général de tactique*, which is why he refers to it as "general." However, he plans to undertake this extensive project titled *A Complete Course of Tactics*. He even provided a detailed outline of this work, which he had never written. The book would begin with an analysis of the political systems of all European countries, totaling 34. Each country's domestic politics would be evaluated concerning the previously mentioned factors, while their foreign policies would be analyzed concerning one another. Only after this would the various elements of military science be addressed: "Elementary Tactics" would cover the different branches of the military, while "Great Tactics" would focus on marching, combat deployment, and encampment.[181]

Although Guibert may not have developed a definitive universal military system, his doctrinal writings greatly impacted the evolution of warfare. He introduced innovative concepts such as mobility, speed, and daring in operations, along with using local resources to address logistical issues. His advocacy for independent movement formations, akin to Marshal Broglie's proto-divisional system, and the adoption of flexible maneuvers in open columns, as opposed to the rigid linear formations perfected by the Prussians, were groundbreaking. These ideas became part of the evolving French military thought during the final years of the *ancien régime*, shaping the doctrines of the French army just before the Revolution. Guibert's principles formed the foundation of the 1791 Ordinance, which guided the Revolutionary armies into battle, and his *Essai* significantly influenced Napoleon's military education. After the Revolutionary Wars and into the Napoleonic era, military thinkers began reassessing new experiences and challenges. Yet,

---

[180] Gat A. (1989). *The Origins of Military Thought from the Enlightenment to Clausewitz*, pp. 41–42. Oxford University Press.
[181] Gat A. (1989). *The Origins of Military Thought from the Enlightenment to Clausewitz*, p. 46. Oxford University Press.

they continued to frame their analyses using the theoretical ideals spread across Europe by the prominent French Enlightenment military thinkers. In Germany, these ideals were adopted by military theorists from the *Aufklärung*, initially a small, French-influenced provincial group. Over time, however, they applied these concepts in transformative and innovative ways.[182] While thinking about creative ways, I remembered a famous Italian filmmaker, Federico Fellini.

In Fellini's iconic film *La Dolce Vita* (1960), the protagonist, Marcello, attempts to write a novel. He plans to spend the afternoon working on it at a seaside restaurant, where he encounters Paola, a young waitress from Perugia. She plays Perez Prado's cha-cha "Patricia" on the jukebox, later humming to its melody. Marcello asks her whether she has a boyfriend, then likens her to an angel in Umbrian artwork.

In the final moments of *La Dolce Vita*, Paola, the young waitress from the seaside restaurant in Fregene, calls out to Marcello across an estuary. However, the words they exchange are lost in the wind, drowned by the crashing waves. Marcello signals that he cannot hear or understand her and, with a shrug, turns back to the party. One of the women joins him, and they walk away from the beach, holding hands. In a lingering close-up, Paola watches Marcello with an enigmatic smile as she waves at him.[183] Marcello and his group then, move toward their queer house of porno amusements, bringing the film to its unsettling end. This marks the conclusion of one of Federico Fellini's masterpieces.

Federico Fellini's cinematic works often depict a world of alienation and fragmentation, where social transformation seems impossible. In his films, the metaphor of "closed doors" symbolizes his view of a society resistant to change, where engagement with societal forces is futile. His surreal imagery highlights the isolation of individuals in a rapidly evolving world.

Now, let me explain a few important paragraphs in Ayşe Zarakol's Book, *After Defeat: How the East Learned to Live with the West*. However, in the subject-matter of my book, we necessarily need Chapter 6: "Conclusion, Zealots or Herodians?" Ayşe Zarakol was inspired by the historian and

---

[182] Gat A. (1989). *The Origins of Military Thought from the Enlightenment to Clausewitz*, pp. 52–53. Oxford University Press.

[183] *Wikipedia*, "La Dolce Vita." <https://en.wikipedia.org/wiki/La_dolce_vita>.

philosopher Arnold Toynbee (1889–1975) regarding the meaning of these concepts. Zealots or Herodians are not being of the West, not being modern, not being industrialized, secular, civilized, Christian, or democratic. She has brought forward a new understanding of IR that goes beyond constructivism and the theories of English Universities. John Lewis Gaddis's book "The Landscape of History" similarly adopts a multi-perspectivist approach and describes how historians swing back and forth between time and space, structure and process, causation and contingency.

Unlike Fellini, Ayşe Zarakol adopts a more open stance toward social change, represented by the metaphor of "opening doors." Rather than retreating from societal challenges, Zarakol advocates for critical engagement and the possibility of transformation. Her approach emphasizes participation, dialogue, and the active shaping of society's future. In other words, Zarakol has been inspired by Arnold Toynbee, and she always argued about keeping the ways open for democracy and liberalism. Does the contrast between Fellini's "closed doors" and Zarakol's "open doors" reflect a fundamental difference: Fellini's resignation to societal constraints versus Zarakol's belief in the potential for renewal and transformation?

Bibliography

Akkoyunlu, K. (2007). *Military Reform and Democratisation: Turkish and Indonesian Experiences at the Turn of the Millennium.* Adelphi Paper no. 392. London: Routledge/IISS.

Arbatov, G. (1973). *The War of Ideas in Contemporary International Relations.* Moscow: Progress Publishers.

Aron, R. (1968). *Peace and War: A Theory of International Relations.* Translated by R. Howard & A. Baker Fox. New York: Doubleday.

Atay, F. R. (1969). *Laicism in Çankaya, 1981–1938.* Istanbul: Doğan Kardeş Yayınevi.

Atay, F. R. (1999). *Çankaya.* Çağdaş Matbaacılık ve Yayıncılık.

Aydinli, E. (2002). "Between Security and Liberalization: Decoding Turkey's Struggle with the PKK," *Security Dialogue,* 33 (2), 209–225.

Batur, M. (1985). *Anılar ve Görüşler* [Memoirs and Opinions]. Istanbul: Milliyet Yayınları.

Bland, D. L. (2001). "Patterns in Liberal Democratic Civil-Military Relations," *Armed Forces & Society,* 27 (4), 525–540.

Bland, D. L. (2004). "Your Obedient Servant: The Military's Role in the Civil Control of Armed Forces." In H. Born, K. Haltiner, and M. Malesic (eds), *Renaissance of Democratic Control of Armed Forces in Contemporary Societies,* pp. 25. Baden-Baden: Nomos Verlag.

Born, H., Haltiner, K. & Malesic, M. (eds) (2004). *Renaissance of Democratic Control of Armed Forces in Contemporary Societies,* pp. 110. Baden-Baden: Nomos Verlag.

Bozeman, A. B. (1971). *The Future of Law in a Multicultural World.* Princeton: Princeton University Press.

Brodie, B. (1973). *War and Politics.* London: Cassell.

Brown, L. C. (ed.) (1996). *Imperial Legacy: The Ottoman Imprint on the Balkans and the Middle East.* New York: Columbia University Press.

Burk, J. (2002). Theories of Democratic Civil-Military Relations. *Armed Forces & Society,* 29 (1), 15.

Burke, E. (1826). *Works* (Vol. VIII). London.

Cevizci, A. (2010). *Felsefe Sözlüğü*. Istanbul: Paradigma.

Cizre, Ü. (2004). "Democratic Control of Armed Forces on the Edge of Europe: The Case of Turkey." In H. Born, K. Haltiner, and M. Malesic (eds.), *Renaissance of Democratic Control of Armed Forces in Contemporary Societies*, pp. 113. Baden-Baden: Nomos Verlag.

Cohen, R. (2001). "Cooperative Security: From Individual Security to International Stability." In R. Cohen, and M. Mihalka (eds.), *Cooperative Security: New Horizons for International Order*. The Marshall Center Paper no. 3, April, pp. 3.

Coker, C. (2002). *Globalization and Insecurity in the Twenty-first Century: NATO and the Management of Risk*. Adelphi Paper 345. London: IISS.

Cottey, A., Edmunds, T., and Forster, A. (2002). "The Second Generation Problematique: Rethinking Democracy and Civil-Military Relations," *Armed Forces & Society*, 29 (1), 31–56.

Daase, C., and Davis, J. (eds.) (2015). *Clausewitz and Small War*. Oxford: Oxford University Press.

Davison, A. (1998). *Secularism and Revivalism in Turkey: A Hermeneutic Reconsideration*. New Haven and London: Yale University Press.

de Visscher, C. (1970). *Théories et Réalités en Droit International Public* (4th edn.). Paris: Pedone.

Doğan, N. (2018). *Osmanli-Habsburg Savaşlarında bir General: Raimondo Montecuccoli ve Tercüme-i Fenn-i Harb (1660–1664)*. Hacettepe University, History Department, M.A. Thesis.

Dürrenmatt, P. (1958). "La Fondation de l'Etat Fédératif," *Histoire de la Suisse: la Confédération et l'État Fédératif*. Payot.

Erickson, E. J. (2007). *Ottoman Army Effectiveness in World War I*. New York and Canada: Routledge.

Erickson, E. J., and Uyar, M. (2009). *A Military History of the Ottomans: From Osman to Atatürk*. Oxford: Oxford University Press.

Feaver, P. D. (1996). "The Civil-Military Problematique: Huntington, Janowitz, and the Question of Civilian Control," *Armed Forces & Society*, 23 (2), 149–178.

Financial Times (2006). October 14–15, 1–2, 6.

Findley, C. V. (1996). "The Ottoman Administrative Legacy and the Modern Middle East." In L. C. Brown (ed.), *Imperial Legacy: The Ottoman Imprint on the Balkans and the Middle East*, pp. 158. New York: Columbia University Press.

Finnemore, M. (1996). "Constructing Norms of Humanitarian Intervention." In P. J. Katzenstein (ed.), *The Culture of National Security*. New York: Columbia University Press.

Gaddis, J. L. (2002). *The Landscape of History: How Historians Map the Past*. Oxford: Oxford University Press.

Gat, A. (1989). *The Origins of Military Thought from the Enlightenment to Clausewitz*. Oxford: Clarendon Press.

Geertz, C. (1973). *The Interpretation of Cultures*. New York: Basic Books.

Goetschel, L. (2000). "Globalization and Security: The Challenge of Collective Action in a Politically Fragmented World," *Global Society*, 14 (2), 276–277.

Göksel, B. (1983). *Hatıra ve Misalleriyle Askeri Tarih'in Milli Eğitim ve Kültürdeki Yeri ve Önemi*. Ankara: Genelkurmay Başkanlığı.

Grunebaum, G. E. (1953). *Medieval Islam: A Study in Cultural Orientation* (2nd edn.). Chicago: University of Chicago Press.

Güvenç, S., and Uyar, M. (2021). "Lost in Translation or Transformation? The Impact of American Aid on the Turkish Military, 1947–1960," *Cold War History*. Available at: <https://doi.org/10.1080/14682745.2020.1866551>.

Hanioğlu, M. Ş. (2008). *A Brief History of the Late Ottoman Empire*. Princeton: Princeton University Press.

Hanioğlu, M. Ş. (2011). *Atatürk: An Intellectual Biography*. Princeton: Princeton University Press.

Hanioğlu, M. Ş. (2023). "Jön Türklerin Bilimciliği ve Bilimcilerin Garpçılığı (Chapter 3)." *Atatürk: Entelektüel Biyografi*. İstanbul: Bağlam Yayıncılık.

Heper, M., and Itzkowitz-Shifrinson, J. R. (2005). "Civil–Military Relations in Israel and Turkey," *Journal of Political and Military Sociology*, 33 (2), 244.

Hourani, A. (1963). "The Decline of the West in the Middle East." In R. H. Nolte (ed.), *The Modern Middle East*, pp. 49. New York: Atheneum.

Hurewitz, J. (1961). "Ottoman Diplomacy and the European State System," *Middle East Journal*, 141–152.

Inbar, E. (2003). *The Israeli–Turkish Strategic Partnership*. Ramat Gan: BESA, Bar-Ilan University.

Itzkowitz, N. (1972). *Ottoman Empire and Islamic Tradition*. New York: University of Chicago Press.

Jenkins, G. (2001). *Context and Circumstance: The Turkish Military and Politics*. Adelphi Paper 337. Oxford: Oxford University Press/IISS.

İnalcık, H. (1973). *The Ottoman Empire: The Classical Age (1300–1600)*. Translated by N. Itzkowitz, and C. Imber. London: Weidenfeld and Nicolson.

İnalcik, H. (1974). The Turkish Impact on the Development of Modern Europe. In K. H. Karpat (ed), *The Ottoman State and Its Place in World History*, pp. 52. Leiden: Brill.

İnalcık, H. (1980). "Turkey between Europe and the Middle East," *Foreign Policy*, 8 (3–4), 7.

İnalcık, H. (2011). *Rönesans Avrupası: Türkiye'nin Batı Medeniyetiyle Özdeşleşme Süreci*. İstanbul: İş Bankası Kültür Yayınları.

İnalcık, H. (2016). *Osmanlı Tarihinde İslamiyet ve Devlet*. İstanbul: İş Bankası Kültür Yayınları.

Karabekir, K. (1969). *İstiklal Harbimiz*. İstanbul: Türkiye Yayınevi.

Karal, E. Z. (1988). *Selim III'ün Hatt-ı Hümâyunları, 1789–1807*. Ankara: Türk Tarih Kurumu.

Karaosmanoğlu, A. L. (1984). "Islam and Its Implications for the International System." In M. Heper, and R. Israeli (eds.), *Islam and Politics*, pp. 103–105. London: Croom Helm; repr. 2013, London and New York: Routledge.

Karaosmanoğlu, A. L. (1993). "Officers: Westernization and Democracy." In M. Heper, A. Öncü, and H. Kramer (eds.), *Turkey and the West: Changing Political and Cultural Identities*, pp. 19–34. London and New York: I.B. Tauris.

Karaosmanoğlu, A. L. (1994). "The Limits of International Influence for Democratization." In M. Heper, and A. Evin (eds.), *Politics in the Third*

Turkish Republic, pp. 117–131. Boulder and San Francisco: Westview Press.

Karaosmanoğlu, A. L. (1999). "NATO Enlargement and the South: A Turkish Perspective." *Security Dialogue*, 30 (2), 213, 221.

Karaosmanoğlu, A. L., and Kibaroğlu, M. (2002). "Defense Reform in Turkey". In I. Gyarmati, and T. Winkler (eds.), *Post-Cold War Defense Reform: Lessons Learned in Europe and the United States*, pp. 157–159. Washington, DC: Brassey's.

Karaosmanoğlu, A. L. (2011). "Yirminci Yüzyılda Savaşı Tartışmak: Clausewitz Yeniden." *Uluslararası İlişkiler*, 8 (29), 5–25.

Karaosmanoğlu, A. L. (2021). "Strateji Düşüncesinde Yorum ve Tahrifat: Clausewitz Olayı." In M. Uyar (ed.), *Savaş Çalışmaları*, pp. 263–268. İstanbul: Kronik Yayınevi.

Karpat, K. H. (1974). "The Stages of Ottoman History." In K. H. Karpat (ed.), *The Ottoman State and Its Place in World History*, pp. 79–98. Leiden: E.J. Brill.

Karpat, K. H. (2001). *The Politicization of Islam*. Oxford: Oxford University Press.

Khadduri, M. (1963). "The Islamic System: Its Competition and Coexistence with Western Systems." In R. H. Nolte (ed.), *The Modern Middle East*, pp. 150–151. New York: Atheneum.

Khadduri, M. (1965.) "The Islamic Theory of International Relations and Its Contemporary Relevance." In J. H. Proctor (ed.), *Islam and International Relations*, pp. 31. New York: Praeger.

Khadduri, M. (1966). *Introduction to the Islamic Law of Nations: Shaybani's Siyar*. Baltimore: Johns Hopkins Press.

Kirişçi, K. (2006). *Turkey's Foreign Policy in Turbulent Times*. Chaillot Paper no. 92, pp. 32–38. Paris: Institute for Security Studies.

Kissinger, H. A. (1974). *American Foreign Policy*. New York: W.W. Norton.

Kuloğlu, A., and Sahin, M. (2006). "The Past and the Future of Civil-Military Relations in Turkey." In S. Faltas, and S. Jansen (eds.), *Governance and the Military: Perspectives for Change in Turkey*. Harmonie Paper, pp. 96–97. Groningen: CESS.

Larrabee, F. S., and Lesser, I. O. (2003). *Turkish Foreign Policy in an Age of Uncertainty*. Santa Monica, CA: RAND.

Lebow, R. N. (2008). *A Cultural Theory of International Relations.* Cambridge: Cambridge University Press.

Leites, N. (1951). *The Operational Code of the Politburo.* Santa Monica, CA: The RAND Corporation; new ed. 2007.

Mantran, R. (1989). *Histoire de l'Empire Ottoman.* Paris: Fayard.

Mango, A. (2000). *Atatürk: The Biography of the Founder of Modern Turkey.* New York: The Overlook Press.

Mardin, Ş. (1971). 'Ideology and Religion in the Turkish Revolution," *International Journal of Middle East Studies*, 2, 198–199.

Mardin, Ş. (1981). Atatürk and Positivist Thought. In *Atatürk and Turkey of the Republican Era.* Ankara: Turkish Union of Chambers.

Mardin, Ş. (2005). "Turkish Islamic Exceptionalism Yesterday and Today: Continuity, Rupture and Reconstruction in Operational Codes," *Turkish Studies*, 6 (2), 145–165.

Mardin, Ş. (2006). *Religion, Society, and Modernity in Turkey.* Syracuse, NY: Syracuse University Press.

McNeill, W. H. (1974). "The Ottoman Empire in World History." In K. H. Karpat (ed), *The Ottoman State and Its Place in World History*, pp. 34–35. Leiden: Brill.

Morse, E. L. (1976). *Modernization and the Transformation of International Relations.* New York: Basic Books.

Oğuzlu, H. T., and Güngör, U. (2006). "Peace Operations and the Transformation of Turkey's Security Policy." *Contemporary Security Policy*, 27 (3), 472–488.

Outwaite, W. (1994). "Hans-Georg Gadamer." In Q. Skinner (ed.), *The Return of Grand Theory in the Human Sciences*, pp. 34. Cambridge: Cambridge University Press.

Özbudun, E. (1996). "The Continuing Ottoman Legacy and the State Tradition in the Middle East." In L. C. Brown (ed.), *Imperial Legacy: The Ottoman Imprint on the Balkans and the Middle East*, pp. 133–157. New York: Columbia University Press.

Özcan, G. (2020). "Türkiye'de Milli Güvenlik Kavramının Gelişimi ve Ulusal Strateji Arayışları." In A. L. Karaosmanoğlu, and E. Aydınlı (eds.)

Strateji Düşüncesi: Kuram, Paradoks ve Uygulama, pp. 123–144. İstanbul: Bilgi Üniversitesi Yayınları.

Paret, P. (2009). *The Cognitive Challenge of War: Prussia 1806*. Princeton and Oxford: Princeton University Press.

Parvin, M., & Sommer, M. (1980). "Dar al-Islam: The Evolution of Muslim Territoriality and Its Implications for Conflict Resolution in the Middle East," *International Middle East Studies*, 1–21.

Perlmutter, A. (1978). *The Military and Politics in Modern Times*. New Haven, CT: Yale University Press.

Radu, M. (2001). "The Rise and Fall of the PKK," *Orbis*, 45 (1), 47–63.

Rogstad, A. (2022). "Stigma Dynamics and the Crisis of Liberal Ordering," *Global Studies Quarterly*, 1–11.

Ruggie, J. G. (1996). *Winning the Peace*. New York: Columbia University Press.

Rustow, D. A. (1958). "Foreign Policy of the Turkish Republic." In R. C. Macridis (ed.), *Foreign Policy in World Politics*, pp. 313. Englewood Cliffs, NJ: Prentice Hall.

Sayegh, F. A. (1966). *The Zionist Diplomacy*. Beirut.

Scheipers, S. (2018). *On Small War: Carl von Clausewitz and People's War*. Oxford: Oxford University Press.

Schiff, R. L. (1995). "Civil–Military Relations Reconsidered: A Theory of Concordance." *Armed Forces & Society*, 22 (1), 7–24.

Shaw, S. J. (1976). *History of the Ottoman Empire and Modern Turkey: The Rise and Decline of the Ottoman Empire, 1280–1808*. Cambridge: Cambridge University Press.

Shaw, M. (2001). "The Development of the Common Risk Society." *Society*, (September/October), 7.

Skirbekk, G., and Gilje, N. (1999). *Felsefe Tarihi*. Translated by E. Akbaş, and Ş. Mutlu. Istanbul: Kitapevi.

Steinbrunner, J. D. (2002). *Principles of Global Security*. Washington, DC: Brookings Institution.

Stern, B. (2001). "How to Regulate Globalization." In M. Byers (ed.), *The Role of Law in International Politics*. Oxford: Oxford University Press.

Stone, N. (2004). "Turkey in the Russian Mirror." In J. Erickson (ed.), *Russia: War, Peace and Diplomacy*, pp. 86–102. Great Britain: Weidenfeld and Nicolson.

Strachan, H. (2006). "Making Strategy: Civil-Military Relations after Iraq," *Survival*, 48 (3), 67.

Strachan, H. (2007). "Clausewitz and the Dialectics of War." In H. Strachan, and A. Herberg-Rothe (eds.), *Clausewitz in the Twenty-First Century*. Oxford: Oxford University Press.

Strachan, H. (2008). "Strategy and the Limitation of War," *Survival*, 50 (1), 34.

Taylor, C. (1985). *Philosophy and the Human Sciences*. Cambridge: Cambridge University Press.

Taylor, C. (1989). *Sources of the Self: The Making of the Modern Identity*. Cambridge, MA: Harvard University Press.

Taylor, C. (2016). "Charles Taylor Has Reimagined Identity and Morality for a Secular Age," *LSE* (London School of Economics), London. <https://blogs.lse.ac.uk/southasia/2016/10/19/charles-taylor-has-reimagined-identity-and-morality-for-a-secular-age/>.

Tocqueville, A. (2002). *Democracy in America*. Chicago: University of Chicago Press.

Toprak, B. (1988). "The State, Politics and Religion in Turkey." In M. Heper, and A. O. Evin (eds.), *State, Democracy and the Military: Turkey in the 1980s*. Berlin and New York: de Gruyter.

Tuathail, G. O. (1999). "Understanding Critical Geopolitics: Geopolitics and Risk Society." In C. S. Gray, and G. Sloan (eds), *Geopolitics: Geography and Strategy*, pp. 107–124. London: Frank Cass.

Turam, B. (2007). *Between Islam and the State: The Politics of Engagement*. Stanford, CA: Stanford University Press.

Uyar, M., and Erickson, E. J. (2019). *A Military History of The Ottomans from Osman to Atatürk*, pp. 1–128.

Uyar, M., and Karaosmanoğlu, A. L. (2020). "Türkiye Askeri Yüksek Öğretimine Strateji ve Güvenlik Çalışmalarındaki Değişimin Yansımaları: Kara Harp Okulu Örneği." In A. L. Karaosmanoğlu, and E. Aydınlı (eds.), *Strateji Düşüncesi*, pp. 313–334. İstanbul: Bilgi Üniversitesi Yayınları.

Vali, F. A. (1971). *Bridge Across the Bosporus: The Foreign Policy of Turkey*. Baltimore and London: The Johns Hopkins University Press.

van Eekelen, W. (chairman), and Greenwood, D. (rapporteur) (2005). *Turkish Civil-Military Relations and the EU: Preparation for Continuing Convergence*. Final Report of a Task Force, pp. 12. Groningen: CESS.

von der Goltz, C. (2012). In F. Yılmaz (ed.), *Yirminci Yüzyıl Başlarında Osmanlı-Alman İlişkileri*. İstanbul: İz Yayıncılık.

von der Goltz, C. (2016). *Millet'i Müselleha (Ordu Millet—Das Volk in Waffen)*. Prepared for publication by İ. Sarıbal.

von Grunebaum, G. E. (1962). *Modern Islam: The Search for Cultural Identity*. Berkeley: University of California Press.

William, O. (1994). "Hans-Georg Gadamer." In Q. Skinner (ed.), *The Return of Grand Theory in the Human Sciences*, pp. 34. Cambridge: Cambridge University Press.

Yetkin, M. (2006). "Gül: Askerlerin AB Desteğinden Memnunuz [Gül: We are Happy with the Military's Support to the EU Project]," *Radikal*, 15 June, p. 6.

Yurdusev, N. (2004). "The Ottoman Attitude toward Diplomacy." In N. Yurdusev (ed.), *Ottoman Diplomacy: Conventional or Unconventional*, pp. 5–30. London: Palgrave Macmillan.

Zarakol, A. (2011). *After Defeat: How the East Learned to Live with the West*. Cambridge: Cambridge University Press.

Zelikow, P. (2003). "The Transformation of National Security: Five Redefinitions," *National Interest*, 71(Spring), 17–28.

Index

www.ingramcontent.com/pod-product-compliance
Lightning Source LLC
Chambersburg PA
CBHW030245100426
42812CB00002B/319